Cocktails
with My Cat

Cocktails with My Cat

TASTY TIPPLES
FOR FELINE FANATICS

Natalie Bovis

Illustrated by Rae Ritchie

RUNNING PRESS
PHILADELPHIA

Running Press
Hachette Book Group
1290 Avenue of the Americas, New York, NY 10104
www.runningpress.com
@Running_Press

Printed in China

First Edition: April 2024

Published by Running Press, an imprint of Hachette Book Group, Inc.
The Running Press name and logo are trademarks of Hachette Book Group, Inc.

The Hachette Speakers Bureau provides a wide range of authors for speaking events.
To find out more, go to www.hachettespeakersbureau.com
or email HachetteSpeakers@hbgusa.com.

Running Press books may be purchased in bulk for business, educational, or promotional use.
For more information, please contact your local bookseller or the Hachette Book Group
Special Markets Department at Special.Markets@hbgusa.com.

The publisher is not responsible for websites (or their content)
that are not owned by the publisher.

Print book cover and interior design by Frances J. Soo Ping Chow.
Stock illustrations on pages 2 and 4 copyright © Getty Images/Anna Suslina

Library of Congress Control Number: 2023941945

ISBNs: 978-0-7624-8410-2 (hardcover), 978-0-7624-8411-9 (ebook)

APS

10 9 8 7 6 5 4 3 2 1

I dedicate this book to my mom, whose own volunteerism
inspires me to help those in need, and to my niece, Ava.

· ·

Throughout *Cocktails with My Cat*, I aim to spotlight how lucky
we are to share this beautiful planet with other intelligent, emotional,
sentient species and emphasize our responsibility to protect them.

· ·

Additionally, this book honors animal rescuers, fosterers,
adopters, veterinarians, shelter staff, donors, and volunteers as well as
the many cats I've loved . . . and the many still to come.

Contents

HOW BETTER TO CELEBRATE THE FINELY TUNED
FELINE ART OF DOING NOTHING THAN BY HAVING
COCKTAILS WITH MY CAT?

—THE LIQUID MUSE

Introduction

CATS ARE ELEGANT CREATURES AND COCKTAILS ARE SOPHIS-
ticated little drinks, and so I think they go well together. Even if you're lounging
at home in your comfies with only your feline furbaby for company, a cat and a
cocktail make any situation just a little bit fabulous. Much of this book was written
with at least one of my five cats on my lap, lolling in a patch of sun, or tiptoeing
across my computer. At times, I also had a cocktail in hand to get my own creative
juices flowing while developing the recipes throughout the coming pages. I had so
much fun researching the many interesting cats you'll read about, and I'm excited
to share them with other cat lovers like you!

I didn't adopt my first dog until my forties when a certain black pup stole
my heart while I was volunteering at a shelter. Lula taught me about the deep

connections between humans and canines, and she inspired my previous book *Drinking with My Dog.* Before Lula, I liked dogs although I didn't fully understand them. With cats, though, there was always just an instinctive connection.

Cats are magical, mystical, clever, cunning, and downright hilarious sometimes. Any cat lover will tell you they are as affectionate and intelligent as dogs and they can learn words, perform tricks, and even play fetch. Like us, cats communicate with their eyes and facial expressions, body language, and sounds. While dogs are eager to please people, cats please themselves—and we can't help but admire them for it! If I'm making analogies, a dog could be your friendly neighborhood beer slinger while a cat is more like the fancy-pants mixologist in a too-hip-for-the-masses trendy bar.

On the following pages, you'll meet all kinds of cats, and each entry is punctuated with its own delicious cocktail recipe. There is a section on creating and stocking your home bar for *purrrfect* cocktail making. There is kitty trivia about wildcats, working cats, famous felines, cool cats of every variety, and a plethora of cat ladies—and gents! You'll even get tips to create a signature cocktail in honor of your favorite feline.

My dream is to share a delicious drink with like-minded animal advocates and create more conversation around wildlife preservation, environmental protection, and continued action against animal abuse. Whether as household pets or majestic beasts roaming hidden corners of the Earth, these beautiful felines rely on *us* to protect them and their surroundings. With a clink of a glass and the swish of a tail, we can stir up more interest in animal conservation while shaking up cocktails in our home bars with our furry friends by our side.

WHEN WE LOOK AT THE WORLD THROUGH
ANOTHER ANIMAL'S EYES, WE HAVE TO REALIZE THAT,
INSIDE, WE'RE ALL THE SAME—AND SO WE ALL DESERVE
TO LIVE FREE FROM SUFFERING.

—JOAQUIN PHOENIX,
AMERICAN ACTOR

I LOVE CATS BECAUSE I ENJOY MY HOME;
AND LITTLE BY LITTLE, THEY BECOME ITS VISIBLE SOUL.

—JEAN COCTEAU,
FRENCH WRITER AND FILMMAKER

YOUR HOME BAR

SHARING IS CARING WHEN IT COMES TO COCKTAILS, AND

while it's stating the obvious that these cocktails are intended for your cat-loving human friends, please don't serve them to your precious kitties. With that in mind, welcome to the wonderful world of mixology! You don't need to be an expert in the kitchen or have bartending experience to make great drinks. You can create a charming home bar whether you are decorating a cart in the corner of your living room or turning your basement into the neighborhood watering hole. With a few bottles of spirits, a smattering of liqueurs, a cocktail shaker, and some fun glassware, you can show everyone that you are king or queen of the jungle when it comes to mixology.

Below, you'll find a list of all the glassware you'll need if you're a serious home bartender looking to round out your collection. Don't fret if you don't have the funds or space for everything. Even if you served every drink in this book in a paper cup, they would still taste delicious. If you do get into the spirit of collecting, though, I suggest perusing virtual or in-person flea markets and resale stores for cool vintage pieces. Also, keep an out eye out for animal shelter thrift stores. Many rescue groups take donations of gently used clothing, glassware, furniture, and other household items to sell in their own secondhand market stalls or their own shops. The money from sales helps pay for food and vet bills. Who doesn't love shopping for a good cause?

Below, I've listed glassware, bar tools, and ingredients in case you're ready to go all out, but don't let these lists intimidate you. If you have a mason jar (instead of a cocktail shaker), a glass (of any kind), a tray of ice, some liquor, sugar, and lemons or limes, you can make the drinks in this book.

BAR MUG   CHAMPAGNE FLUTE   COCKTAIL COUPE   HIGHBALL GLASS   COCKTAIL GLASS   RED WINE GLASS   ROCKS GLASS   WHITE WINE GLASS

BAR MUG • A thick glass with a handle for cold or warm drinks.

CHAMPAGNE FLUTE • A long, narrow stemmed glass used for sparkling drinks.

COCKTAIL COUPE/COCKTAIL GLASS • The original wide-bowled Champagne glass which is now used more often than not for classic stirred cocktails.

HIGHBALL/COLLINS/TALL GLASS • Ideal for fizzy drinks, with the Collins being a bit taller than a highball, which usually holds just a spirit plus mixer.

MARTINI/COCKTAIL GLASS • This V-shaped cocktail glass holds every variation of "tini" drink you can think of; traditionally called a cocktail glass.

RED WINE GLASS • A goblet with a large surface area allowing for more oxygen to react with the wine, thereby allowing the flavors to open.

ROCKS/DOUBLE ROCKS GLASS • A short, wide glass used for sipping spirits served neat/"up" or "on the rocks"—no ice and with ice, respectively. Obviously, the double rocks holds a bit more liquid than the plain rocks glass.

WHITE WINE GLASS • A smaller, tulip-shaped wineglass.

LAP IT UP

When serving cocktails, the glass is an important part of the over-all drinking experience. We taste first with our eyes, so presentation counts. And, in proper cocktail-making etiquette, some drinks call for a specific type of glass. As you get into cocktail making, collecting beautiful stemware can become an obsession. I had to cut myself off from buying vintage cocktail glasses in much the same way I had to cut myself off from adopting more pets! Just as a little furry face pulls at my heartstrings, an early 1900s Champagne coupe or a mid-century gold-rimmed cocktail glass has me convincing myself that "just one more" is still not enough.

KITCHEN TOOLS AND APPLIANCES

BLENDER • For blending frozen cocktails.

CUTTING BOARD AND PARING KNIFE • For cutting fruits and veggies.

GRATER • For grating ginger, nutmeg, and chocolate, for instance, and for zesting citrus peels.

ICE CUBE MOLDS • Look for trays with fun shapes or larger openings. Larger cubes melt more slowly. When making ice blocks for a punch bowl or pitcher, use a small plastic tub such as a yogurt or cottage cheese container. You can also use tonic water or juice in place of plain water to further flavor the punch as it melts rather than water it down.

JUICER • Freshly juiced fruits and vegetables make for more delicious cocktails.

MEASURING CUP • For measuring batched drinks.

PEELER • For taking the skins off fruits and veggies; helpful for making lemon or lime twists.

SMALL SAUCEPAN • For cooking syrups or purees.

BASIC BAR TOOLS

| BARSPOON | CITRUS PRESS | COCKTAIL SHAKER | ICE SCOOP | JIGGER | MUDDLER | SIEVE |

BARSPOON • Used to stir drinks, a barspoon has a long stem, and measures about 1 teaspoon, or ¼ of an ounce.

CITRUS PRESS • This handheld kitchen tool is shaped like half an orange, lemon, or lime and easily squeezes out juice while holding back seeds.

COCKTAIL SHAKER • These can be both decorative and functional. A three-piece shaker has the strainer built in. A professional set of shaker tins has a larger and smaller tin that seal when shaking liquid. A Boston shaker has a tin which fits over the mouth of a pint glass. I like using these in my cocktail classes because the students can see the ingredients as they go into the glass, making it easier to follow along. Next, we add ice and seal it up with the metal tin over the top before shaking. We use a Hawthorne strainer—a round, slotted metal lid with a spring in it to hold back ice and other solids—to pour the liquid into the glass.

ICE SCOOP • When you put out a bowl of ice at a party, you will need to provide an easy and sanitary way for people to scoop it into their glass.

JIGGER • Measures liquids in ounces or milliliters.

MUDDLER • Made from wood, plastic, or metal, a muddler is essentially a pestle with a long handle to reach the bottom of a cocktail shaker and is used to press the juice or oils from fruits and herbs.

SIEVE • If you are shaking berries or muddling herbs, you might want to double strain your drink. Hold a small sieve above the cocktail glass to catch little bits of mint leaves or berry seeds as the contents of the shaker go through it so they don't get stuck in your teeth when you take a sip.

INGREDIENTS

BAKING SPICES • Some of the recipes in this book call for spices, including cinnamon, cloves, or nutmeg.

CITRUS FRUITS • Limes, lemons, oranges, and grapefruits are just a few of the fruits you'll find in the recipes in this book.

CREAM • Typically, drinks use heavy cream, but half-and-half can be substituted for anyone watching their fat intake. For those who prefer nondairy, coconut creamer is a good substitute.

EGGS • Egg whites and egg yolks are used in a variety of drinks as they add texture, mouthfeel, or froth. If you're looking for a vegan substitute for egg whites in cocktails, try aquafaba or garbanzo bean water. See page 15 for notes about adding raw eggs to drinks.

FRESH HERBS • Mint, basil, and thyme are most common in cocktail recipes, although you'll find many recipes using other herbs, too.

FRUITS AND VEGGIES • Just about any produce can be used in drinks, making for more fresh and flavorful beverages.

SEA SALT • For rimming glasses. See page 15 for a note about rimming glasses.

SUGAR • Granulated white or raw is ideal for making syrups; note some vintage cocktail recipes call for a whole sugar cube or lump.

THE LIQUID KITTY

Just as the word *kitty* can be used for a coffer to store gold, your home bar can be a treasure trove of liquid delights when you show off your newly honed cocktail skills. And you'll find yourself making frequent deposits from your favorite liquor store. Personally, I love bringing back an unusual spirit or liqueur from a trip to sip with friends while sharing travel stories—and photos of the cats I met—in faraway destinations. Whenever I land somewhere new, I try to understand how the people there eat as well as how they drink. It's a peek into that culture's local customs, tastes, and values. Also learning to make delicious things abroad is a very tactile way to share your experiences with your peeps back home.

Below is a list of spirits and other ingredients to create a foundation for your home bar. If this is new to you, don't get overwhelmed because you do not need to have all these things to get started. If you're on a budget, buy bottles in increments. And, if you are particularly limited on space or funds, here is a little insider tip: For just about any cocktail you can substitute vodka in place of the spirit the recipe calls for. So, if you can only buy one bottle for now, make it vodka and add more spirits to your home bar as you can.

DISTILLED SPIRITS

Let's demystify alcohol so that you can walk into a liquor store or shop online with confidence. Keep in mind that "more expensive" does not always translate to "better quality." If you shop at a store that has knowledgeable clerks to help you choose the right product for you, that's even better. The following list gives you an overview of the spirits used in this book, including what they're made from and what they might taste like.

BRANDY • A distilled spirit made from grapes. The most famous kind of brandy is Cognac, which is produced in a specific region in France. Others include brandy de Jerez from Spain and pisco, a South American brandy specifically made in Peru and Chile.

CACHAÇA • A form of Brazilian rum made from fermented sugarcane juice versus molasses.

GIN • In short, we can say that gin is juniper-infused vodka, because it can be made from any base as long as juniper is included with the citrus peels, spices, botanicals and flowers distillers choose to create interesting flavors. There are a few distinct gin styles you can try:

London Dry Gin: Heavier in juniper flavor and tends to be a bit "drier" than other styles. It has citrus notes and contains no added sugars.

Modern Gin: Tends to be lighter on the juniper and may include floral and fruity notes.

Sloe Gin: Essentially a liqueur rather than a gin, despite its name. It is sweetened and infused with sloe berries, which are somewhat like a small plum or damson.

RUM • Typically made from molasses, rum can be light (un-aged) or dark (aged in wood for additional flavor and color). Spiced rum has been infused with spices and vanilla. Rum can be made anywhere in the world and remains a very popular spirit in highballs, classic cocktails, and tiki drinks.

TEQUILA • Agave plants can grow in many dry climates, but true tequila is only made from the Blue Weber agave plant and produced in one of the five tequila regions in Mexico. Tequila makers procure used wooden barrels from American Bourbon distilleries, French Cognac makers, and sometimes wineries or Spanish sherry makers to age the spirits. When any spirit sits in a wooden barrel, it gets a deeper brown color from the wood, and its taste mellows. With the explosion of tequila's popularity in the last decade, tequileros are getting more creative with their methods and making more unique products. The following are kinds of tequila you will find on store shelves and descriptors referring to how much time they spent in a barrel. In any spirit category, an older spirit is not necessarily better, but aging will affect its flavor. And never buy a tequila with the word "gold" on the bottle as that usually means that it has been artificially colored.

Blanco means the tequila looks clear in the bottle because it has not been aged. That said, a blanco can be aged in a wooden barrel for up to two months.

Reposado means the tequila has rested in a wood barrel for about two to twelve months.

Añejo means "aged," and the distilled liquid has been aged in the barrel for one to three years.

Extra Añejo means it has been aged in the barrel for longer than three years.

VODKA • Defined as an odorless, tasteless spirit, vodka can be made from any grain, vegetable, or fruit—not just from potatoes, as some believe. There are even vodkas that are made from milk! The base material influences each vodka's mouthfeel and subtle taste. A vodka that is distilled many times is not necessarily a marker of quality, but merely indicates how many times the liquid was put through the distillation process.

WHISKEY • This is a big spirits category, and there are several kinds of whiskey made from different kinds of grain from all corners of the world. Note there are rules pertaining to specific whiskey styles, some of which are briefly outlined below. You'll also notice that sometimes the word *whiskey* is spelled *whisky* depending on where the spirit is made.

Bourbon: Made in the United States from a grain mash that is at least 51 percent corn and aged for at least two years in new charred oak barrels.

Canadian Whisky: Usually a blend that includes rye and is aged for at least two years.

Irish Whiskey: Must be made in the Emerald Isle and aged for three years in wood barrels.

Japanese Whisky: Typically made from barley, like Scotch, but experimentation is expanding in this newer and exciting category.

Rye Whiskey: Has a spicy kick to it and is the style of whiskey called for in many of the original whiskey cocktail recipes.

Scotch is made from malted barley in Scotland.

FORTIFIED WINE

Wine is fortified when it is dosed with a little spirit added along with herbs and botanicals. It is integral to some of our most iconic cocktails, such as Martinis and Manhattans. Like other kinds of wine, some fortified wines are made with specific grapes and are typical of the Mediterranean region, although their rising popularity is encouraging winemakers in other parts of the world to experiment with fortified wines as well. Lighter fortified wines, such as dry vermouth and some sherries, are lovely *aperitifs*, or "appetite openers." Richer wines, such as port, make wonderful *digestifs* or after-dinner drinks. Keep in

mind that because these are wine-based, they must be refrigerated once opened or they will go rancid. Some fortified wines include:

DRY VERMOUTH • This has a white wine base and is dry (not sweet) with rich botanical flavors. It is most often used with clear spirits or on its own as an aperitif. It is made at wineries around the world.

MADEIRA • These fortified wines are made on the Portuguese island of Madeira, off the coast of the Iberian Peninsula. Some varieties are dry and wonderful aperitifs and some are sweet digestifs.

MARSALA • This Italian fortified wine is made on the island of Sicily and ranges from dry to sweet.

PORT • This rich fortified wine comes from the Douro Valley in Portugal. It is most often red and sweet, although there are some drier, white varietals, too.

SHERRY • This fortified wine is from Andalusia, Spain. It also has dry and sweet varietals.

SWEET VERMOUTH • With a red wine base, it is sweeter than dry vermouth with rich botanical flavors. It is most often used with dark spirits. It can be an aperitif or digestif. Made at wineries around the world.

MORE *MMM* IN YOUR MEOW: LAYERING FLAVORS

Once you have chosen a spirit or fortified wine as your cocktail base, the next step is to layer in flavors with different kinds of modifiers. These ingredients can add sweetness, bitterness, floral notes, fruity notes, or spice. More flavor means more fun for your taste buds. Below are some options to take your cocktail from merely a "good kitty" to "fantastic feline!"

LIQUEURS

A liqueur, or cordial, has a spirit base which is sweetened and flavored. Liqueurs can be herbaceous, fruity, floral, nutty, coffee-flavored, mint-flavored, or chocolate-flavored. They can be chilled and sipped on their own, served over ice, or mixed into a cocktail.

BITTERS

Bitters are flavor enhancers made with high-proof alcohol, bark, herbs, and other botanicals. Bitters were first created as a remedy for stomach ailments when mixed with a little water or sparkling water. In mixology, their use can be compared to a dash of salt in food to boost flavor. A little bit goes a long way. A dash of bitters can enhance a cocktail's aroma, as well, when dotted on the surface of a drink. Keep a bottle of each of the traditional Angostura and Peychaud's on hand if you're into classic cocktails, and experiment with a plethora of flavored bitters that have flooded liquor store shelves in recent years.

FLOWER POWER

Dried, candied, or fresh, edible flowers make beautiful garnishes for cocktails and mocktails. Definitely research any flowers you intend to use to make sure they are fit for human consumption. My faves include citrus blossoms, daisies, dandelions, hibiscus, honeysuckle, lavender, mum petals, pansies, rose petals, and violets.

Often used in Middle Eastern, French, or farm-to-table cooking and baking and found in gourmet stores, flower waters such as rose, orange, jasmine, and lavender have subtle aromas and flavors that work beautifully in light, delicate cocktails, particularly ones with a vodka or gin base.

HEAT IT UP

A few dashes of spicy hot sauces are perfect for drinks that taste better with a bit of a kick, such as the Bloody Mary, Spicy Margarita, or a signature cocktail.

SHRUBS

Shrubs are vinegar-based drinks that hearken back to colonial times. Preserving fruit in vinegar was a common way to store produce for the winter season. Adding sugar to the vinegar solution then diluting it with water or club soda when ready to serve makes it palatable as a drink. In recent years, shrubs have made a comeback as an acidic ingredient in modern cocktails and mocktails.

My basic shrub recipe calls for one cup each of vinegar, sugar, and very ripe fruit. I simplify the process by blending all ingredients for about 10 to 15 seconds to thoroughly mix them up. Then, I let the combined shrub sit in the fridge overnight, strain it, and keep the flavorful liquid in the fridge for up to a week. Here are a few combinations I use often:

CANTALOUPE AND STRAWBERRY WITH APPLE CIDER VINEGAR • Peel and seed the melon, and hull the strawberries.

APRICOT AND LAVENDER WITH WHITE VINEGAR • Cut the apricots open and remove pits, then add a tablespoon of dried culinary lavender per cup of fruit.

MIXED BERRIES AND JALAPEÑO WITH BALSAMIC VINEGAR • Blackberries, raspberries, blueberries, and even cherries are great. Slice and seed one jalapeño per cup of berries.

SYRUPS

Homemade syrups are easy to make and, of course, many ready-made ones come in a variety of flavors in stores and online. The foundation of cocktail syrups is Simple Syrup which has a 1:1 ratio of white granulated sugar to water. To make it, simply dissolve the sugar into the water by heating them on the stove in a saucepan or in the microwave for a few minutes, stirring often, then allowing the mixture to cool. This is also the base to more creative syrups, such as the ones below. You can make any syrup sweeter and more concentrated by mixing two parts sugar to one part water. Get fancy by substituting flavored tea, fruit juice, or even wine for the water to create layers of flavor in a drink without needing to add a lot of ingredients.

FLAVORED SYRUPS • Store-bought varieties available for coffee and soda drinks can be used in cocktails.

FLORAL • To infuse floral flavors into your syrup, simply add a couple of table-spoons of dried flower petals while heating the sugar and water. Refrigerate for several hours, then strain.

HERBACEOUS • For herbal syrups, add fresh or dried mint, thyme, or rosemary leaves while heating the sugar and water, refrigerate for several hours, then strain.

HONEY • If you want honey syrup, mix two parts honey with one part water, heat slightly, then shake or stir to mix well. Cool before using.

ORGEAT • An almond syrup that is used in some classic cocktails. Making your own is rather labor-intensive, so store-bought is preferable.

SPICES • When using spices, such as a few strands of saffron, grated ginger, or turmeric, for example, heat them with the sugar and water, let cool, refrigerate for several hours, then strain.

STORE-BOUGHT AGAVE SYRUP • This is ready to use right out of the bottle as it is quite runny.

GARNISHES

A decorative garnish enhances a drink's presentation, while also lending aroma and flavor to the drinking experience. The garnish should reflect the type of drink and the ingredients in the drink. In other words, a Margarita usually gets a lime wedge garnish because there is lime juice in the drink and a whiff of fresh citrus prepares you for the taste about to hit your tongue.

Lemons, limes, oranges, cherries, onions, olives, candied ginger, or citrus peel (cut into little strips called twists or grated zest), edible flowers, lemongrass stalks, seasonal fruits, and vegetables are all commonly used as drink garnishes.

Drink rimmers count as garnishes, too, and can be made from salt or colored sugar. Add more flavor and flare by mixing ground lavender or chili powder in with the salt or sugar. To rim a glass, simply moisten the edge of the glass with a piece of fruit, syrup, or water, and dip it into a plate sprinkled with the powdered rimming ingredient.

Of course, there are also nonedible garnishes, such as little umbrellas, mini clothespins, and picks or skewers (to hold chunks of fruit), and any other fun little toys or elegantly crafted glass decorations.

Don't forget the ice! By freezing berries or edible flowers into the ice cubes themselves, you can create floating drink decor. Go one step further by freezing fruit juice, tonic water, or tea in ice cube trays, which continue adding flavor to the drink as they melt.

*EGG*CELLENT TIPS

People are sometimes squeamish about using raw eggs in cocktails, but they have been incorporated into recipes dating back to the 1800s and give drinks a rich texture. Egg whites bring a silky quality to a cocktail and add a fluffy white cloud to the surface of the drink, while egg yolks make for a creamy, rich cocktail and are used in classic flips and nogs.

For those rightfully concerned about salmonella, be sure to wash the egg before cracking it open, as the bacteria typically lives on the shell rather than inside the egg itself. And, of course, use eggs, dairy, or any food-based ingredient according to your own risk and judgment.

DRY SHAKE

When shaking egg or cream into a cocktail, the mixture must first undergo a vigorous "dry" shake—i.e., *without* ice—to mix the ingredients and start to make the drink frothy and light. After the dry shake, add ice to the shaker and vigorously shake with the ice again before straining it into a glass.

SHAKE OR STIR?

A basic mixology rule is that if a drink is all liquor, it is stirred rather than shaken. Think: Manhattans, Negronis, Old Fashioneds, Martinis. In anticipation of anyone quoting James Bond famously requesting a Martini "shaken not stirred" in the 1964 movie *Goldfinger*, keep in mind that Bond had to ask for his drink to be shaken because a properly trained bartender would have stirred it. If the drink recipe calls for juice, cream, egg, tea, or other nonalcoholic ingredients, it is always shaken.

When shaking with ice, put enough ice into the shaker so that it is just poking out of the surface of the liquid. Then shake vigorously to both chill and slightly dilute the drink before straining it into a chilled glass for a drink served *up*, or strain over fresh ice for a drink served *on the rocks*. Resist the temptation to "shake and dump"—sloshing the entire contents of a shaker into a glass, ice and all. We want to avoid this because the ice used for shaking is already melting quickly and you'll be left with a watery cocktail—yuck!

"Rolling" a drink is similar to shaking but much less vigorous. Pour the ice and liquid from one mixing glass or tin into another. This is repeated back and forth a few times. This technique is employed when someone wants to mix the ingredients well without watering the drink down too much by shaking.

If a drink has Champagne or other bubbly mixer, pour half of the bubbles into the glass, then shake and pour in all the noncarbonated ingredients before topping up with more bubbles. This mixes the bubbly into the drink without losing carbonation.

MEASURING TIPS

1 barspoon = 1 teaspoon

The juice of ½ lime equals about ½ ounce.

The juice of ½ lemon equals about ¾ ounce.

When batching a drink for a larger quantity, simply translate ounces to cups and keep the same ratios in the recipe.

OUNCES TO MILLILITERS

The recipes in this book are written in ounces. One fluid ounce is equivalent to just under 30 milliliters. Based on this ratio, below is a quick translation for measurements from ounces to milliliters.

½ ounce = 15 milliliters	2 ounces = 60 milliliters
¾ ounce = 20 milliliters	2½ ounces = 75 milliliters
1 ounce = 30 milliliters	3 ounces = 90 milliliters
1½ ounce = 45 milliliters	1 cup = 240 milliliters

"

IT IS IMPOSSIBLE FOR A LOVER OF CATS TO BANISH
THESE ALERT, GENTLE, AND DISCRIMINATING FRIENDS,
WHO GIVE US JUST ENOUGH OF THEIR REGARD
AND COMPLAISANCE TO MAKE US HUNGER FOR MORE.

"

—AGNES REPPLIER,
AMERICAN ESSAYIST

RESCUE ME!

DID YOU KNOW THAT AS OF 2023, THERE ARE AN ESTIMATED 600 million cats on planet Earth? It's even more mind-blowing to learn that over 400 million of those kitties are strays. According to recent reports, about one in three households in the United States has a pet cat, and about a third of those were adopted from shelters. Nearly half of the cats in shelters came from people abandoning them. The heartbreaking reality is that in the US alone, nearly a million healthy, friendly cats are euthanized each year in crowded shelters if not adopted quickly. Spaying and neutering are key to controlling cat populations. Fostering or adopting are also wonderful ways to not only save a cat but complete your family. This chapter features a few of my own rescue cats. To be honest, I could ramble on for pages about each cat I've adopted, so I've tried to be selective! I'm sure you understand because, if you're anything like me, you know that each kitty's tale is what led them home to you.

Black Cat

Is there such a thing as black cat bias? In some countries, superstition decrees that a black cat crossing your path brings bad luck. But in Ireland and much of the United Kingdom, black cats are believed to bring wealth. In Japan, some think they help attract a mate for their single humans. Back in 1916, American suffragists Alice Burke and Nell Richardson adopted a black kitten named Saxon to be the unofficial mascot of women's right to vote as they met with leaders across the country. So why are black cats adopted less often from shelters than cats of other colors? Some researchers note that their facial expressions may be harder to read in online adoption photos, so humans don't connect with them as quickly. This daring drink is in honor of those beautiful kitties who get overlooked for all the wrong reasons and to the adopters who see them as good omens.

- 6–8 ripe blackberries
- 2 ounces vodka
- ¾ ounce blackberry and jalapeño shrub (See shrubs on page 13.)
- ½ ounce blackstrap molasses
- 1 capsule activated charcoal*
- Garnish: pink orchid

Muddle the blackberries in a cocktail shaker. Add the other ingredients and shake with ice. Double strain into a wine goblet filled with fresh crushed ice. Place the orchid on top of the ice.

*Please note that although activated charcoal capsules are sold as alternative medicine, they could pose health risks. Check with your doctor before using. When in doubt, leave it out.

Stray Cat Slush

The swagger of a tomcat strutting down a moonlit alley tells us he is in search of female feline company or a claws-out, screeching fight with a rival. Come what may, he puts on a brave face. Sidestepping a late-night drunkard or two, slipping past the bar staff taking out the evening's garbage, and searching out a half-eaten burger or even a couple of French fries, this guy knows how to survive on the streets. Deep down though, beneath his dusty fur and scarred-up nose, this fella dreams of his own home, a full food dish, and a loving human with a warm lap. This drink is both strong and sweet—perfect for toasting your newly adopted toughie with a soft heart.

- 1 ounce apricot liqueur
- ¾ ounce rye whiskey
- ¾ ounce Cognac
- ¾ ounce spiced rum
- ¾ ounce fresh lemon juice
- Garnish: dried apricots and cherries on a pick

Shake all the ingredients with ice in a cocktail shaker. Strain into a Collins glass filled with fresh crushed ice. Lay a fruit skewer across the rim of the glass.

The Star

My second year at university I picked up the school paper and saw an ad for free kittens. I couldn't resist the temptation and picked out a fluffy gray one I named Ashley. I really had no business getting a pet at that point in my life, but having come from a home full of cats, my little apartment felt empty without one. After I graduated, Ashley and I drove across the desert to start our new life in Los Angeles where I was part of a theater company for about three years. I soon landed a role in *The Collection*, a Harold Pinter play in which the female lead is a fashion designer who often appears onstage with her cat. The director and I decided that employing a live cat would be more noteworthy than using a stuffed animal, so I carted Ashley to the theater every night for the four-week run. Well, Ashley got a fabulous review from one critic who wrote that my performance was somewhat less interesting than hers. Ha! While it was not a shining moment in my own acting career, there was some consolation knowing that my darling Ashley had star power! This drink is a little bitter and a little sweet, like the bittersweet life of an aspiring actress and her scene-stealing cat.

- 2 ounces bitter liqueur
- 2 ounces tonic water
- 1 ounce grapefruit juice
- Dash of grapefruit bitters
- Garnish: grapefruit twist

Pour all the ingredients into a wine goblet, and stir to combine. Add a large ice cube and a twist of grapefruit peel.

Coffee and Cream

In 1998, I moved to Spain to live with my then-boyfriend and his brother Maiol, who, to this day, remains my dear friend. After settling in, I pleaded my case for us to get a *gatito* because, obviously, no home is complete without a cat. For months, the boys were against it as we all three lived in an already too small apartment. However, one day, Maiol surprised me with the most perfect fluffy white and brown kitten whom I delightedly named *Tallat*, the Catalan word for "espresso with a splash of milk." I was thrilled with my new baby and soon brought home a second kitten to keep him company. How could I not? The guy giving away the other little white runt was threatening to drown him in the river if nobody took him. *Tasman* was deaf, as many all-white cats are, with one green and one blue eye, and displayed the personality of a Tasmanian devil. A couple of years later, I moved back to the United States and managed to convince airport authorities to let me board the plane with both of my then huge and very fat cats. My sweet *gatos* lived to be sixteen and fifteen years old, respectively, and saw me through several more moves and several more boyfriends. This cocktail has a coffee and cream base, the spicy swirl of a mischievous demon, and a hint of Spanish flare.

- 1½ ounces Spanish brandy
- 1 ounce espresso
- 1 ounce cream or milk
  (or nondairy equivalent)
- ¾ ounce cinnamon liqueur
- Garnish: whipped cream and
  ground cinnamon

This drink can be served warm or cold. If serving cold, shake all ingredients with ice in a cocktail shaker and strain into a Martini glass. If serving warm, add a second shot of espresso and serve in a heat resistant mug.

Saintly Soul Mate

A soul mate is someone with whom you have an instant connection who under-stands you without words and immediately feels like family. I believe we have many soul mates—and these can include lovers, friends, and animals. My sweet Santo found me at a campsite where friends were preparing their outdoor wedding. The groom-to-be was cooking elk stew in the commissary kitchen and I was standing in the doorway when in walked an enormous, emaciated, dark-chocolate brown cat who slinked up and rubbed my leg. When my eyes locked with the pleading yellow beams shooting from that too-big-for-his-body head, he meowed with hunger. I gave him some scraps and whispered, "If you're still here when I leave, I'm taking you with me," intending to bring him to the shelter. Later, when I coaxed him into my car, I thought perhaps he should have a hearty meal first. At my house, he ravenously fell upon the food and water. I figured he could also use a good night's sleep before being surrendered to a noisy shelter. By morning, I had to admit out loud that I was not taking that cat anywhere. Of all my cats—and I adore each and every one of them—I had an otherworldly connection with Santo. He'd crawl up on my chest and look deep into my eyes outpouring gratitude every day until he died from heart failure only a few years later. Before his passing, I started fostering kittens again. Santo took a particular liking to a lone, struggling three-week-old gray tabby and snuggled that baby into health. I keep a framed photo of giant Santo head-to-head with baby Caillou who is now eight years old. This chocolate cocktail is in honor of Santo, the saintly soul who knew even before I did that we were meant for each other.

- 2 ounces chocolate vodka
- 1½ ounces chocolate liqueur
- ¾ ounce raspberry liqueur
- Dash of chocolate bitters
- Garnish: raspberries on a pick

Stir all the ingredients with ice in a cocktail shaker, then strain into a chilled coupe. Lay skewered raspberries across the rim of the glass.

YOUR CAT'S GOLDEN YEARS

Just like humans, pets slow down as they age. They require more rest and are prone to achy joints. Your older kitty may need you more than ever to help with life's basics. They may require gentle brushing if they can't groom themselves as well as they once did. They may prefer softer food or help getting to their favorite high-up sunny spot if they can no longer jump. And because they are more fragile, be cautious of rambunctious kittens jumping on them or children handling them roughly. If your older kitty is getting a weaker bladder, you might line their bed with a puppy pee pad. Sadly, shelters receive an abundance of senior kitties when their humans lose patience. But these last years of your cherished cat's life are precious, and just a few small adjustments can make them more comfortable for both of you. Also if you're looking to adopt a new pet, consider a senior cat! They are calm and easy housemates for the most part and will be eternally grateful for a soft place to land for their golden years.

Foster Fail Flip

Fosters are indispensable when shelters and rescues are overflowing with animals who are injured, motherless babies arrive, or pets are displaced during natural disasters. I began fostering neonatal kittens at my good friend's rescue in Spain when I moved back there temporarily in 2010. I filled my new apartment with bottle-feeder babies who needed kitten formula every few hours, a rub on their backsides to facilitate bowel movements, and lotsa love to bond with humans. After weeks of intense nurturing comes the tearful task of bringing healthy, adorable floofs back to the shelter or rescue hoping they'll find forever homes. It is a satisfying endeavor if you don't get too attached! When I returned to the United States, I continued fostering. The temptation, once I was in my own house, was that I didn't *have* to give them back, did I? Within a month of adopting Caillou, I "foster failed" two more tabby kittens, brothers Cocoa and Marmalade. With three new kittens, I was careening toward a cat-adoption intervention! So I took a break from fostering kittens and decided to walk shelter dogs instead. (If you have my previous book, *Drinking with My Dog*, you know how that brilliant idea turned out!) Here's a drink for all the other failures like me who "flip" for felines. A *flip* in cocktail lingo means including rich egg yolk. This drink honors both Cocoa and Marmalade who completed my trio of tabbies.

- 1½ ounces spiced rum
- 1 ounce chocolate liqueur
- ¾ ounce heavy cream
- 1 teaspoon orange marmalade
- 1 teaspoon cocoa powder
- 1 raw egg yolk (optional)
- Garnish: a pinch of cocoa powder on the surface of the drink

Dry-shake all the ingredients— remember a dry shake means no ice— vigorously for at least 30 seconds in a cocktail shaker. Add ice and shake vigorously again. Strain into a Martini glass and sprinkle with a pinch of cocoa powder.

Kindness Is Glamorous

When does an obsession with cat videos become animal activism? When you're following two social media sensations like Beth Stern and Kitten Lady Hannah Shaw! Model Beth Stern shares not only the softer side of her shock jock hubby Howard Stern on her popular Instagram @bethostern, but she also fosters and rehomes rescue kitties year-round through her charitable foundation Beth's Furry Friends. Followers fall in love with each kitty she helps, heals, and guides into a new family. Often her adopters start their own Instagram accounts so Beth's fans can continue following the lives of their favorite cats with their new families. Kitten Lady Hannah Shaw has over a million followers on Instagram, where fans are regaled with adorable kitten pix and vids of her rescues @kittenxlady. She also started her own nonprofit benefiting cats, has written many books about kitties, and was named 2019 Cat Advocate of the Year by the ASPCA. In addition to the lifesaving work these high-profile advocates do, they also raise awareness on a global level. This glammy drink can be made as a cocktail or mocktail, and like both women's generous souls, it sparkles in more ways than one—beautiful inside and out.

- ¾ ounce cherry liqueur (or substitute with cherry juice if making a mocktail)
- 2 pinches of edible gold cocktail glitter
- 3 ounces Champagne (or substitute with nonalcoholic sparkling wine if making a mocktail)
- Garnish: gold-dusted cherry

Pour the cherry liqueur or juice and one pinch of gold cocktail glitter into a coupe or white wine glass. Slowly add the Champagne. Sprinkle the cherry with a second pinch of edible gold cocktail glitter and drop it into the drink.

OF ALL GOD'S CREATURES, THERE IS ONLY ONE
THAT CANNOT BE MADE SLAVE OF THE LEASH. THAT ONE IS
THE CAT. IF MAN COULD BE CROSSED WITH THE CAT, IT WOULD
IMPROVE THE MAN BUT IT WOULD DETERIORATE THE CAT.

—MARK TWAIN,
AMERICAN AUTHOR

CHAPTER
3

WORKING CATS

ALTHOUGH CATS SEEM TO HAVE US WRAPPED AROUND THEIR little paws and catering to their every whim, when they want to they can pull their own weight in a variety of ways. First, cats are proven to be good for their human's mental health. Their soft fur is soothing to the touch, which helps us to relax. And is it even possible to look at a kitten without our hearts feeling like just-out-of-the-oven warm and gooey chocolate chip cookies, all sweet and melty? Additionally, cats' calming purrs have been proven to lower people's blood pressure. Beyond these obvious benefits, people who have figured out how to harness cats' many talents by respecting their unique personalities rather than trying to force them into submission can utilize their superior skills. Cats are efficient hunters, easy-going companions, and natural entertainers. The cats in this chapter excel at their jobs and, let's face it, even the idea of a cat agreeing to perform a service rather than lounging around and simply being served by its human is toastworthy in and of itself.

CLICK CAT

Did you know that cats can be trained with a clicker just like dogs and horses? It may take a few weeks—and a whole bunch of your kitty's favorite treats—but cat cooperation is just clicks away. Every time you say a command and your cat does what you ask, make the clicking sound and provide a delicious reward. The key is to click and treat immediately when they do what you ask so that they associate the noise and pleasurable consequence with compliance. If even cats can be trained with clickers, it begs the question: Would clicks and treats work for human domination, too?

AS ANYONE WHO HAS EVER BEEN AROUND A CAT FOR
ANY LENGTH OF TIME WELL KNOWS, CATS HAVE ENORMOUS PATIENCE
WITH THE LIMITATIONS OF THE HUMANKIND.

—CLEVELAND AMORY,
AMERICAN AUTHOR AND ANIMAL RIGHTS ACTIVIST

Performing Poofballs

In 2018, the Ukrainian Savitsky family's performing cats became a sensation on the TV show *America's Got Talent*, and they have since been booking high-paying gigs for other shows and private events. The feline superstars jump through hoops, walk upright on hind legs, jump off high poles onto handheld cushions, and display their exceptional balance in gravity-defying tricks. To train these gorgeous, long-haired rescue kitties, the Savitskys invest many hours, lots of affection, and buckets full of treats. Acknowledging that even their exceptional felines won't be coaxed into doing tricks unless they decide they want to, the show's routines are designed around each cat's particular likes or physical abilities. As they travel around delighting audiences, these cats have become beloved feline ambassadors for their country. Although not specifically related to the Savitsky cats, it is worth mentioning that Ukraine is also home to a rare European wildcat that lives in its mystical forests. In honor of the special felines in Ukraine as well as the resilient people who live there, this drink is layered yellow and blue to reflect the colors of the Ukrainian flag.

- 2 ounces pineapple juice
- 1½ ounces vodka
- 1 ounce blue curaçao
- Garnish: lemon wedge

Shake the vodka and pineapple juice with ice in a cocktail shaker and strain into a Martini glass. Slowly, pour in blue curaçao so that it can create a layered effect. Place the lemon wedge on the rim of the glass and decorate the drink with a mini blue and yellow flag.

Scarlett the Brave

A mother's job is to care for her babies, and mama cats take this as seriously as humans. In 1996, a young homeless cat gave birth to five kittens in a garage allegedly used as an illegal drug house in Brooklyn. When firefighters responded to a fire in that garage, they noticed a mama cat dashing back into the flames to carry her kittens out one by one. Her paws, ears, and fur were severely burned and her eyes were blistered over. She blindly nudged each kitten before collapsing from smoke inhalation and injuries. One of the hero firefighters took the little family to a vet where one kitten died but the rest, including the mama, recovered. This mother's bravery made international headlines and got over 7,000 requests for adoption. The babies were adopted out in pairs, and Scarlett found a loving home where she lived until her passing in 2008. Her story was so touching that it inspired a book as well as the North Shore Animal League's Scarlett Award for Animal Heroism. This cocktail honors Scarlett and all the homeless kitty mamas caring for their little ones.

- 1½ ounces vodka
- 1½ ounces ruby red grapefruit juice
- ¾ ounce cranberry syrup (equal parts cranberry juice and sugar) (See page 14.)
- ½ ounce fresh lime juice
- Garnish: lime wheel

Shake all the ingredients with ice in a cocktail shaker and strain into a Martini glass. Slide the lime wheel onto the rim of the glass.

Amelia the Tropicat

When Liz Clark first met the kitty who would become the first mate aboard her boat, the cat was a scrawny, hungry youngster about six months old. On that fateful day in 2013, California-born Captain Liz was living a nomadic life on the ocean, sailing, surfing, and exploring coastlines. She wasn't looking to adopt a pet. However, as these things go, something about this cat stuck in her soul, so she named her Amelia after the adventuring Ms. Earhart. The high-energy kitty adjusted to living on a small sailboat but still yearned to explore the jungles and would often venture off into the wilds when the boat was docked. She was a highly intelligent being—like all cats—who caught bugs to entertain herself on the boat, joined Liz on beach walks, and was even a good enough swimmer to take a dip then get herself back on board via a cloth ladder. She was often the star of Liz's travel writing. In Tahiti, Liz started a nonprofit called A Ti'a Matairea whose animal welfare mission includes sterilizations funded by the French Fondation Brigitte Bardot, reporting domestic and wild animal abuse, and finding escorts to take homeless animals abroad for adoption. Amelia has since passed away, but we can raise a glass to her unique lifestyle.

- 2 ounces dark rum infused with Tahitian vanilla bean (Slice a bean or two, place in bottle, let stand at least a week.)
- ½ ounce butterscotch syrup
- Dash of walnut bitters
- Garnish: dehydrated pineapple with mini paper clip

Pour the ingredients into a double rocks glass and stir. Add a large ice cube and attach the pineapple to the rim of the glass.

Mighty Mouser

Mother Nature is wiser than us all, and every animal has a purpose in our ecological balance. People have always benefited from cats controlling the rodent population, particularly the ones that carry diseases. Unfortunately, during the Middle Ages, religious leaders blamed the world's ills on sorcery and witchcraft and often associated cats with evil forces. Due to this negative propaganda, many cats were cruelly exterminated, and when the bubonic plague began to expand along trade routes, cats were wrongly blamed for spreading the disease. In reality, the illness was carried by rodents, and because people were encouraged to kill cats, the diseased rats ran wild and one-third of Europe's human population died. This drink is a riff on the Last Word made with a monastic botanical liqueur to honor those mighty mousers that could have reduced the 25 million death toll had they not been wrongly defamed by men of the cloth.

- ¾ ounce yellow Chartreuse
- ¾ ounce gin
- ¾ ounce fresh lemon juice
- ¾ ounce apricot liqueur
- Garnish: dried apricot

Shake all the ingredients with ice in a cocktail shaker and strain into a coupe. Garnish with the apricot.

Thank You for Your Service Cats

If your cat has curled up next to you when you've been in bed with the flu or zonked out from a long day, you can attest that cats are natural empaths who pick up on human feelings. These emotional benefits have helped cats become generally recognized as official emotional support and companion animals with a doctor's note so that they can be allowed places where pets normally can't go. Nevertheless, the Americans with Disabilities Act does not include cats on its list of official service animals. This seems a bit unfair as cats can be taught a variety of duties. For example, in 2006, a cat named Tommy made headlines when he saved his paralyzed human's life because he had been trained to dial 911 after his person began to regularly suffer fainting spells. Pets for Patriots is an organization that mainly provides dogs to assist injured veterans with daily duties, but they also recognize that cats can help alleviate PTSD and depression. Still, even when a cat is providing emotional support to their human, only the person is covered under the ADA, not the hardworking kitty. In honor of the cats helping humans through challenges in life, we can petition the ADA to recognize cats for these jobs. Meanwhile, let's have a patriotic drink made with Bourbon—America's spirit—in their honor.

- 1½ ounces Bourbon
- 1 ounce spiced apple cider
- 1 ounce ginger beer
- ¾ ounce fresh lemon juice
- Garnish: apple fan made from thin slices of apples

Pour all ingredients into a Collins glass. Add crushed ice, stir, and place the apple fan on the surface of the drink.

Downward Cat

One year, I gave myself the gift of a yoga retreat in Ibiza. At each morning session, a small black kitty slunk into the garden where our teacher guided the group through physical movements and mental relaxation. Unable to stop my monkey mind from swinging from thought to thought—and being interested in meeting animals when I travel—I would creep my eyelids open during meditation to look for the daily visitor who'd gratefully sidle up to the water and dry food left for her outside the patio door. Apparently, she belonged to nobody in particular, and she wandered the neighborhood hoping for hospitality. At first, I wondered if I should take her to a shelter with hopes of finding her a permanent home. But was I just imposing my expectations onto her? She looked very healthy and, frankly, happy. A shelter would be a stressful environment, while here she had a network of homes providing her food. She had trees to climb and empty pool chairs to lounge upon. As I tossed these ideas around, the content kitty sat silently across the garden looking at us, the humans seeking the kind of peace she lived day in and day out. Perhaps permanence wasn't the reward I thought it was. I mentally thanked the kitty yogi who unknowingly imparted the deepest lesson of the week. This mocktail mingles spicy tea with sweet fruit and is a nod to the lessons we learn from animals.

- 3 ounces chai, brewed (warm or cold)
- ¾ ounce banana syrup
- ¾ ounce whole milk (or nondairy milk)
- Garnish: banana slices sprinkled with ground anise or cinnamon on a skewer

This drink can be served warm or cold. If serving warm, pour all the ingredients into a bar mug and stir. If serving cold, shake all the ingredients with ice in a cocktail shaker and then strain into a Martini glass.

Seven Seas and Six Toes

Sailors have long considered cats good luck, and until 1975, the British navy kept cats on ships. Warship cats sometimes even had their own little hammocks, and in 1943, the US Coast Guard gave one cat named Herman the Mouser his own ID. Going back a bit further, cats prowled the decks of Spanish galleons and plundering pirate ships feasting on stowaway rats and mice. Being tossed about on enormous waves could prove tricky business for the felines so *polydactyls*—cats with six toes—were particularly popular. The extra claw helped them hang on, climb, and be very effective hunters. During the time of great trade between the New England colonies and Great Britain, there was a rise in the polydactyl cat population. Today, cats with this inherited trait are most commonly found along the East Coast of the United States, Canada, South West England, and Wales. They are less commonly found in Europe because false rumors associated their extra toe with witchcraft, so zealots hunted and killed them. Today, if you want to meet a six-toed feline, you can visit Ernest Hemingway's former home, now a museum on Key West. The dozens of polydactyls in residence are said to be descended from a white six-toed cat given to the author by a ship's captain. Perhaps the perfect drink to honor these special kitties is my variation on the Gin and Tonic, a classic highball that originated from British sailors mixing their gin rations with quinine-rich tonic to stave off malaria and squeezing in lime juice to prevent scurvy.

- 3 ounces tonic water
- 1½ ounces London Dry gin
- ½ ounce Amontillado sherry
- Garnish: lime wedge

Fill a Collins glass with ice, then pour in half the tonic water. Add the gin and sherry and stir, then add the rest of the tonic water. Place the lime wedge on the rim of the glass.

Guardian of the Grain

As you read in the first chapter of this book, some spirits are made from grain such as barley, rye, wheat, and corn. The first step in making spirits from grain is fermenting it into a beer. Once alcohol has been created through that process, the beer is distilled to extract the alcohol. From there, it is aged in wood barrels. So, if rodents eat the grain or otherwise contaminate it, there is no booze! Enter the all-important distillery cat. This feline career has been around since humans began gathering extra food to store for lean times. Cats hear very high frequencies and so are adept at tracking mice and other little creatures by their squeaking. Being able to locate and remove the rodents means cats can protect the grain used to make the liquor. Mice tend to be more active when it is dark and humans are out of sight, so cats' crepuscular tendencies, making them most active at dawn and dusk, are well suited for the job. One famous Scottish feline named Towser is credited with killing an average of three mice per day, or over 28,000 in her lifetime!

- 2 ounces Scotch
- ¾ ounce almond or hazelnut liqueur
- ½ ounce amaro
- Garnish: lemon twist

Stir all the ingredients with ice in a mixing glass and pour over fresh ice in a double rocks glass. Express the oil from the lemon twist over the surface of the drink, then drop it in.

Bodega Rebel

In Spanish, a *bodega* refers to a wine cellar. In New York City, people use the word to refer to a corner store that carries daily life staples such as groceries, hot morning coffee, and sometimes a full deli. Bodegas are a hubbub of daily life in the Big Apple, so it's no wonder kitties are drawn to the action. Sometimes bodega cats are pets, and sometimes they are neighborhood strays who adopt the community on the block. In the United States, health laws don't allow live animals to go into food stores, so having a bodega cat means that the establishment risks a fine. Still, the penalty for mice or other rodents found in the store costs even more. Therefore, many shopkeepers choose to let a friendly block cat hide out inside their store especially when winter temperatures take a dive. In honor of the cats who warm the hearts of the many customers who love bodega cats, as seen on social media accounts dedicated to these hardworking felines, this drink tastes like a cozy, creamy hug.

- 3 ounces steamed milk (or nondairy milk)
- 2 ounces brandy
- ¾ ounce anise liqueur
- Garnish: cinnamon powder

Pour all the ingredients into a heat resistant mug and sprinkle with cinnamon powder.

WHEN I AM FEELING LOW, ALL I HAVE TO DO
IS WATCH MY CATS AND MY COURAGE RETURNS.

—CHARLES BUKOWSKI,
AMERICAN AUTHOR

CHAPTER
4

COOL CATS

IN THIS CHAPTER, I'M SHARING A FEW CATS WHO HAVE

unique stories or traits as well as some interesting breeds. Of course, the coolest cat of all is one who has been *rescued!* I don't advocate breeding animals for profit because there are so many beautiful mixed-breed cats sitting in shelters worldwide just hoping for a home. Still, in a cat lovers' book, it is fun to explore the different looks, traits, sizes, and fur patterns kitties can have. When it comes to fancy-pants cats, the International Cat Association recognizes 73+ cat breeds, and there are over 400 licensed cat shows that happen around the world each year. One difference between cat and dog shows is that cats are bred to display unusual aesthetic features, whereas dog breeds are designed to excel at particular tasks. The result of this genetic tinkering means that there are twice as many dog breeds as cats, but there remains a huge range of diversity within cat populations. Pour yourself a tasty drink as we dive in to explore some cool kitties and what makes them so noteworthy.

THAT CUTE LITTLE SNORE COULD BE TELLING YOU SOMETHING . . .

The adorable smoosh-faced purebred kitties may have sought-after looks, but those very characteristics can be deadly. Just as with pugs and bulldogs, flat-faced cat breeding is problematic because their "purr-wheezing" can indicate BAS or brachycephalic airway syndrome. Pets suffering from this disease can't get enough oxygen to run and play like healthy animals—those of us with asthma can relate to how hard and scary it can be in a full-on attack, and these poor kitties live this way full-time. Persians, Himalayans, Burmeses, folds, and British shorthairs, among others, are typical cuties who suffer from inbreeding. How can you help reduce the breeding of unhealthy kitties for profit? If you have your heart set on a specific kind of cat, adopt one from a breed-specific rescue.

Copy Cat

When we adopt a pet, we have the honor of loving them from their infancy through their old age. But, what if, when they pass on, we didn't have to say goodbye for good? In 2004, a Texas woman was the first person to hire a California-based biotech company to use the DNA from her deceased Maine coon to create a cloned version of her beloved cat. Of course, only the physicality can be replicated as each cat's personality is unique. Still, when she received the eight-week-old replica of Little Nicky, she said it was worth every penny of the $50,000 bill! Cloning for the masses is still a ways off, but in tribute to this technological marvel, this drink calls for a couple of unusual ingredients, including edible gold leaf.

- 1½ ounces vanilla vodka
- ¾ ounce banana liqueur
- ½ ounce fresh lime juice
- ½ ounce yellow Chartreuse
- Garnish: banana slices topped with edible gold leaf

Shake the ingredients with ice in a cocktail shaker and strain into a coupe or over a large ice cube in a double rocks glass. Place the golden banana slices on the large ice cube or skewer them and lay them on the rim of the glass for an up drink poured into a cocktail glass with no ice.

Kittea Café

If you're longing for some kitty love but don't have a furball of your own, take yourself down to a cat café and cuddle to your heart's content. These establishments bring together two of our favorite addictions—caffeine and felines—and are popping up all over the world! These marvelous places originated in Taiwan and soon caught on in Japan where pets are not always allowed in small apartments. The cat café trend has spread to the United States, Europe, and Australia, and café kitties are often available for adoption. How better to get to know a potential pet than in a relaxed environment while lounging on a sofa rather than the high-stress surroundings of a shelter? This steaming cup of dirty chai yumminess (a *dirty chai* is a latte with a shot of espresso) would go down well alongside an oh-so-cool, cuddle puddle kitty, don't you think?

CATS CHOOSE US; WE DON'T OWN THEM.

—KRISTIN CAST,
BEST-SELLING AMERICAN AUTHOR

- 3 ounces chai
- 2 ounces oat milk, steamed
- 1 ounce espresso
- ¾ ounce cream liqueur
- Garnish: ground nutmeg

Mix all the ingredients in a bar mug and sprinkle with nutmeg.

Hairless Wonder

Furless cats are rare, and the Canadian sphynx is one of the most famous of these kitties. These highly social and talkative cats are very playful, though their sleek, elegant form looks more like a work of art than a pet. They were purposely bred to be bald starting in the mid-1900s. Aside from their unique appearance, this was likely to make them hypoallergenic and convenient pets for people who didn't want to clean hair off their clothes and furniture. They often have a soft peach fuzz covering their epidermis, but without fur to protect them from the sun or cold, they are most comfortable and healthy as indoor cats. And despite not needing to be brushed, their skin still requires special grooming as extra oil can clog their pores. Don't judge these affectionate fellows by their bare skin, however. They are just as cuddly as their furry feline friends, even if they require just a bit more care. This elegant drink features Canadian whisky and maple syrup in honor of these very unique cats.

- 2 ounces Canadian whisky
- ½ ounce maple syrup
- 2 dashes of walnut bitters
- Garnish: candied walnuts

Pour all the ingredients into a double rocks glass, stir, add ice if desired, and serve with candied walnuts on the side.

Tail Tales

The swish of a cat's tail is a communicative gesture that can mean anything from "Come play with me!" to "Stay back, I'm angry!" So what do we know about cats without tails? The British Manx hails from the Isle of Man, and there is also a variation called a Cymric, or long-haired Manx. They usually have round heads and rounded bodies and typically no tail at all due to a genetic mutation. In another part of the world, Japanese bobtails date back to the sixth century and are typified by a triangular head and a little rabbitlike tail. The tricolored bobtails are considered to be good luck, and the Japanese maneki-neko good luck cat statue is actually modeled on this breed. The American bobtail has a little stumpy tail, and its lineage originated in the 1960s but, sadly, had become severely inbred by the 1980s. The Highland lynx was genetically designed in the United States in the mid-1990s by crossbreeding a desert lynx with a Scottish fold resulting in curled ears and a bobbed tail. The small tails on all of these cats are actually very sensitive because they house many nerve endings, so extra caution is required from their humans. In honor of these kitties' tails, this drink is short, tasty, and sure to please just as much as a long one!

- 1½ ounces vodka
- ¾ ounce honey syrup
- ¾ ounce fresh lemon juice
- ½ ounce peach schnapps
- Garnish: lemon wheel

Shake all the ingredients with ice in a cocktail shaker and pour into a Martini glass. Place the lemon wheel on the rim of the glass.

Cat Gods and Goddesses

I could have written a whole chapter—or even a whole book—about cat gods and goddesses. Throughout humanity, felines have played a sacred role in human life. Archaeologists have found cat remains buried with humans as far back as 10,000 BC in Cyprus, and the Greek goddess Hecate is said to have assumed the form of a cat at times. Hieroglyphics tell us that ancient Egyptians worshipped cats and kept them in their homes, although the cats were not "owned." Their queen Cleopatra is said to have had a cat companion called Tivali. Among Egyptian deities, Bastet and Sekhmet were depicted as women with the head of a cat and lion, respectively, and people made offerings at their altars. A Chinese cat god called Li Shou is said to have protected farmers from mice, and Ai-Apaec was a pre-Inca god with fangs and whiskers said to have descended from an even more ancient cat god. The Hindu goddess Durga represents feminine divine feline energy and is said to ride a lion. Similarly, a Semitic goddess known as Asherah or Qadesh was referred to as the Lion Lady. Whether the deity was part feline or had cat helpers, it is clear that kitties have been revered as godlike creatures through millennia, so it's only appropriate to raise a glass to them with this heavenly concoction.

- 4 ounces hibiscus tea
- ½ ounce anise-flavored liqueur
- ¼ ounce rose water
- Garnish: lemon wedge and mint leaves

Shake all the ingredients with ice and strain into a Martini glass. Place the lemon wedge and mint leaves on the rim of the glass.

Gentle Giant

Maine coons are the largest of domestic cat breeds and get their name from the northeasternmost state in the United States. They have luxurious, dense fur that requires frequent brushing to avoid matting and are often marked with little tufts of hair poking out of their ears or between their paws. They are shy around people they don't know but very affectionate with family members. These large cats likely traveled to the American colonies on ships from Europe where large forest cats lived for eons. Their water-repellent coats and large paws would make them excellent ship mousers, after all. To date, the largest pet Maine coon on record was four feet long! These fantastic felines nearly went extinct in the 1950s when cat enthusiasts were seeking Persians, Angoras, and other "plush" house cat breeds. Today, however, Maine coons are among the most sought-after cat varieties and enjoying their time in the spotlight. To toast these fabulous felines, I'm using rye whiskey and cranberry juice, two beverages which also hail from the northeastern United States.

- 1½ ounces rye whiskey
- ¾ ounce cranberry juice
- ½ ounce cinnamon syrup
- ½ ounce fresh lime juice
- Garnish: lime twist

Shake all the ingredients with ice in a cocktail shaker and strain into a coupe. Place the lime twist on the rim of the glass.

Vikings of the Forest

A mysterious and very distinctive large cat originates in Scandinavian forests. Given the sparse daylight in snowy winter months, it is no surprise that these kitties' double-layer fur coats would remain a dominant trait. *Skogkatt*s appear in Norse mythology as favorite companions of the goddess Freyja, which indicates they are woven into the fabric of ancient Northern European culture, although some say they were brought to the region by the Romans. Norwegian forest cats come in all colors but commonly have white bellies and tabby shells. Their ears often have lynx tips—tufts of hair growing from their tops—and they are considered highly intelligent. These are not lap cats—they are far too adventurous—but they are loyal to their human family and enjoy being near them. In 1938, King Olav V declared them the official cats of Norway. While at first they may appear similar to a Maine coon, the forest cats have distinctly different facial features such as a more triangular head. This drink features aquavit, meaning "water of life." It is commonly drunk in Scandinavia and similar to gin but highlights caraway rather than juniper.

- 2 ounces aquavit
- 1½ ounces grapefruit juice
- ¾ ounce elderflower liqueur
- Garnish: grapefruit peel

Pour all the ingredients into a double rocks glass. Add ice and stir. Either lay a strip of grapefruit peel on the rim of the glass or grate a little zest over the surface of the drink.

Bengali Sour

Did you know that 95 percent of domestic cat DNA is similar to that of tigers? We cat lovers can't help but be enchanted with the idea of a bit of wildcat existing within the purring pal sleeping on our sofas. Perhaps the thought that they could wake up one day and make breakfast of us is enthralling on some subconscious level? Enter the Bengal cat, a result of breeding small Asian leopards with a house cat. These cats have slender, muscular bodies and golden coats spotted with rosettes and sometimes a marbled appearance. They have often been crossed with the Egyptian mau, a domesticated spotted kitty. A reference to this mixing of Asian leopard with pet cats first appears in a book called *Our Cats and All About Them* published in the late 1880s and reprinted in more recent years. The proliferation of Bengals in the United States began in the 1970s, and eventually the breed was accepted into cat associations around the world over the next 20 years. Due to their wild ancestry, Bengals have unique characteristics such as a fondness for water and retrieving or playing fetch. And also because of their wildcat heritage, they are banned or restricted in many states and countries. In honor of these tiny tigers, this drink has a sake base and bright fruit flavors.

- 2 ounces nigori sake
- 2 ounces honeydew melon juice (or any preferred melon juice)
- 1 ounce yuzu puree
- ¾ ounce green tea syrup
- 1 egg white (optional)
- Garnish: melon balls

Dry-shake all the ingredients in a cocktail shaker. Add ice and shake vigorously again. Strain into a coupe or Martini glass. Drop the melon balls in the drink or skewer them across the rim of the glass.

Fold & Rag

The Scottish fold's rounded head, soft fur, and huge owllike eyes melt the hearts of cat lovers. This breed originated in Scotland, supposedly from a barn cat named Susie in the 1960s. Also known as the Highland fold, their cute appearance and friendly disposition have made them extremely popular around the world, particularly in the United States and Asia. Sadly, though, their signature folded ears are due to feline osteochondrodysplasia, a genetic condition affecting cartilage and bone. Overbreeding worsens this condition and causes the cat to suffer painful arthritis. In the 1970s, the United Kingdom stopped registering folds for cat shows over concern for their well-being. This Scotch-based drink is deliciously sweet and bitter in honor of these furbabies.

- 1 ounce Scotch
- 1 ounce cherry liqueur
- 1 ounce amaro
- 1 ounce orange juice

Shake all the ingredients with ice in a cocktail shaker and strain over fresh ice in a rocks glass.

The Coolest Cat in Hollywood

In 2012, a shy mountain lion was discovered nimbly surviving in Griffith Park, a patch of nature surrounded by Los Angeles freeways, where thousands of people hike, bike, and picnic every year. He was fitted with a radio collar to track his movements and became a symbol of the plight of wildlife as cities and humans encroach upon their longtime habitats. He was the subject of books and documentaries, and there is a famous photograph of him slinking along a mountain ridge at night with the Hollywood sign shining brightly beyond. Because of the dangerous freeways, he lived alone and was unable to venture farther afield to find a mate—his isolation tore at the hearts of animal lovers. Mountain lions are nocturnal hunters, and in 2022, the starving cat attacked a Chihuahua when its human took it for a nighttime stroll in the hills. Twelve-year-old P-22 was soon captured and euthanized. Reports say he was frail and had sustained injuries from a car strike. His passing reminded me of one of my favorite poems about the rivalry between wildlife and human society, so this excerpt from D. H. Lawrence's "Mountain Lion" leads us seamlessly into the next chapter about wildcats:

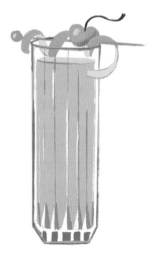

> *And I think in this empty world*
> *   there was room for me*
> *and a mountain lion.*
> *And I think in the world beyond,*
> *   how easily we might*
> *spare a million or two of humans*
> *And never miss them.*
> *Yet what a gap in the world,*
> *   the missing white frost face*
> *of that slim yellow mountain lion.*

Let's raise a glass to this Hollywood legend with a frosty, golden cocktail in his honor.

- 3 ounces Sauvignon Blanc wine (or alcohol-removed white wine)
- 1 ounce pineapple juice
- ¾ ounce grapefruit juice
- ½ ounce passion fruit syrup
- Garnish: lemon twist and a cherry

Put all the ingredients with a big handful of ice in a blender and mix for about 30 seconds until smooth. Pour into a Collins glass and place the lemon twist and cherry atop the frozen drink.

CATS KNOW HOW TO OBTAIN FOOD WITHOUT LABOR, SHELTER WITHOUT CONFINEMENT, AND LOVE WITHOUT PENALTIES.

—W. L. GEORGE,
BRITISH NOVELIST

THE GREATNESS OF A NATION CAN BE JUDGED
BY THE WAY ITS ANIMALS ARE TREATED.

—MAHATMA GANDHI,
INDIAN LAWYER, ANTICOLONIAL NATIONALIST,
AND POLITICAL ETHICIST

CHAPTER
5

WILDCATS

OF THE 600 MILLION MEMBERS OF THE FELIDAE–OR LITHE-
bodied carnivorous mammals—across the globe, 100 million are wildcats. The
Panthera genus of cats includes five main big cat groups: lion, tiger, jaguar, leopard,
and snow leopard (with snow leopard more closely related to a tiger than leopard).
There are over 40 species of small undomesticated felines, and most of those are
dotted across all continents except Antarctica. It is difficult to be certain which is
the rarest wildcat on Earth because we simply don't know enough about the elusive
felids who hide in the remotest parts of the planet. In this chapter, we will learn a
little more about the shy wildcats who deserve both reverence and protection. Big
cat lovers can take action to protect these incredible beings, most of whom are on
the brink of extinction, by supporting wildcat rescues and antipoaching groups.

Big Love, Small Package

The rusty-spotted cat may fit in the palm of your hand but make no mistake: it is a tiny version of a wild leopard and absolutely should not be kept as a pet. As kittens they weigh less than a chicken egg, have rust-colored sides with white bellies, white lines around their eyes, and will eventually develop spots on their backs. As adults, they can weigh about two pounds, have big eyes, rounded ears, and black pads on their feet. They are nocturnal with vision six times more powerful than a human and mainly live in the shrinking wet forests of India, Sri Lanka, and some parts of Nepal. To pay tribute to the rusty-spotted cat, this drink is a twist on the classic Rusty Nail, which is said to have been a favorite of the 1960s Rat Pack—Frank Sinatra, Dean Martin, Sammy Davis Jr., among others. It is made from Scotch and a honeyed botanical whiskey-based liqueur.

- 2 ounces Earl Grey tea
- 1½ ounces Scotch
- 1 ounce Drambuie

Shake all the ingredients with ice and strain over fresh ice in a double rocks glass. If you prefer to make this a hot drink, add more tea and serve it in a heat resistant bar mug or teacup.

Bay Breeze

The Borneo Bay cat is found only on its namesake island. Its presence was first recorded in 1874 by British zoologist John Edward Gray, and this wildcat remains as mysterious today as it was then. It is genetically linked to two other Asian cats—the golden and marbled cats—who likely shared a common ancestor about five million years ago. These cats are very rarely seen in the wild but have recently been caught on cameras as they flee logging and palm oil farms. They cannot survive without lush forest, and tragically Borneo has one of the highest deforestation rates on the planet. I chose the Bay Breeze to honor this cat purely because of its name, but the highball actually has an interesting history of its own. When cranberry producers wanted to promote the juice in the mid-1900s, a slew of new cranberry juice cocktails hit bars around the United States. Clearly, it worked because, today, every American bar keeps cranberry juice in its refrigerator.

- 2 ounces pineapple-flavored vodka
- 2 ounces pineapple juice
- 2 ounces cranberry juice
- Garnish: cherry and orange slice

Pour all the ingredients into a highball or Collins glass, then add ice. Drop the cherry and orange slice into the drink or skewer them and place on the rim of the glass.

El Tigre

Just over a hundred years ago, 100,000 tigers roamed evergreen and tropical rain forests, mangrove swamps, grasslands, and savannas. Today, due to poaching, as few as 4,000 wild tigers are spread across Bangladesh, Bhutan, Cambodia, China, India, Indonesia, Laos, Malaysia, Myanmar, Nepal, Russia, Thailand, and Vietnam. These beautiful beings also lost 95 percent of their territory to human activity. No South China tigers have been seen since the late 1980s, and island tigers on Java and Bali have been eradicated while only a few remain on Sumatra. Unlike most house cats, tigers love water and are fantastic swimmers. They almost always travel alone, except for mothers and their cubs, so protecting one tiger requires conserving 25,000 acres of forest. Tigers are great hunters and can take down animals five times their own body weight, which is handy because with the average tiger weighing 220 to 650 pounds, they can eat up to 88 pounds of meat at one time! The average tiger has more than 100 stripes, yet no two tigers have the same stripe pattern. This drink is based on an Indian lassi and features delicious tropical ingredients. Without the alcohol, it makes a great mocktail, too.

- ½ cup fresh or frozen mango chunks, peeled
- ½ cup yogurt
- ¼ cup milk or coconut milk (adjust as needed for thicker or thinner drink)
- 2 ounces gin
- 1 pinch cardamom
- 1 pinch ground cinnamon
- Garnish: crushed pistachio nuts and coconut flakes

Blend all the ingredients in a blender with a couple of ice cubes to the desired consistency. Pour into a wine goblet or Collins glass. Sprinkle with crushed pistachios and coconut flakes.

Spot Me If You Can

Margays are among the most beautiful of the spotted cats and live all the way from Mexico through Central and South America, predominately in tropical and subtropical evergreen areas. The margay resembles the larger ocelot so much that in some parts of South America it is referred to as "little ocelot." However, margays avoid areas where ocelots live because of prey competition. This negative effect on other small cat populations is called the "ocelot effect" due to the smaller cats being forced into areas where the threat of human interaction is greater. The margay population has decreased owing to this, as well as poaching for their pelts and the illegal pet trade. When left in their habitats, margays live and hunt easily in cloud forests due to their long tails, broad feet, and strong toes by which they can hang. They descend trees headfirst, whereas most other cats climb down feetfirst. Their diet consists of small rodents, reptiles, and birds. In some places bursting with small primates, such as Costa Rica, they are also known to eat monkeys. These clever cats have even been recorded imitating the call of a baby tamarin monkey to lure in and ambush the adults. This drink mimics the margay in that it is a bit daring and thoroughly delicious, pulling inspiration from the Americas.

- 1½ ounces cachaça
- ¾ ounce passion fruit puree
- ½ ounce fresh lime juice
- ½ ounce orange liqueur
- Garnish: lime wheel

Shake all the ingredients with ice in a cocktail shaker and strain into a Martini glass or serve over fresh ice in a Collins glass. Slide the lime wheel onto the rim of the glass.

The Pride of Africa

African lions are very social big cats living in prides of about 15 members. Females often give birth around the same time so cubs can nurse from multiple mothers. The protective male lion's roar can be heard from five miles away, and they always eat first even though the females do most of the hunting. Despite being called "king of the jungle," lions mainly live in grassy plains, though some adaptable fellows wander beaches in Tanzania and the desert in Namibia. More fun facts about lions: They only have a 30 percent success rate when hunting. They walk on tippy-toes with their heels never touching the ground. A male lion's mane darkens as he grows older. And they are one of only three big cats that roar. It's crazy to think that in the mid-1900s, there were about 450,000 wild lions. Today, there are only 3,000 roaming free in Africa and 12,000 in captivity around the world. Tragically, heartless trophy hunters primarily from Europe, North America, and Australia along with a market for lion body parts in Africa and Asia have decimated their population. In 2022, the Oklahoma City Zoo announced the birth of four African lion cubs for the first time in two decades. This unique drink featuring fermented palm tree sap is a tribute to these magical creatures and the preservationists trying desperately to protect them.

- 1½ ounces dark rum
- 1½ ounces fresh orange juice
- 1 ounce palm wine (can substitute dry vermouth)
- ¾ ounce cassis or black currant syrup
- Garnish: orange zest and pinch of ground cinnamon

Shake all the ingredients with ice in a cocktail shaker and strain into a Martini glass if serving up or over fresh ice if serving in a Collins glass. Grate the orange zest and add a pinch of cinnamon across the surface of the drink.

PRESERVATION TOURISM
SAVES WILD ANIMALS

For decades, big cat populations have dwindled due to blood sport and kidnapping them from the wild for illegal trade. Canned hunting is when wild animals are bred and their offspring are raised with the sole purpose of being shot at in an enclosed environment from which they can't escape. Sadly, this is legal in the United States even though animal advocates encourage governments worldwide to ban these cruel activities. Luckily, some countries are leading by example. When the African country of Namibia became independent in 1990, environmental protection and conservation were written into its constitution. This has resulted in growing populations of lions, cheetahs, and other native species within its borders. In response, wildlife lovers have bolstered tourism because they can see these protected animals living in the wild, which in turn contributes to the country's economy. This upward spiral is a win for everyone. The best way to protect animals is through education—the World Wildlife Fund shares online teaching tools about our planet's magnificent animals for families and schools interested in raising a new generation of conservationists.

Snow Ghost

Of all the big cats, leopards are the only ones known to live in both deserts and rain forests in ranges spanning from Africa and Asia to the Middle East and Pacific Ocean. Leopards—even pure black ones—have spots, or rosettes, which help them camouflage for their own protection and to ambush prey. Although they look similar to cheetahs, the two cats are quite different, and the leopard can only run about half as fast as its spotted friend. The Amur leopard, also known as the Manchurian or Korean leopard, is one of the rarest wildcats and lives in the Russian Far East. They can run over 35 miles per hour and jump nearly 20 feet horizontally and 10 feet vertically. Unfortunately, only about 50 individuals are thought to be left in the wild. Snow leopards live in some of the harshest conditions in the world, high up in snowy mountain ranges in China as well as India, Nepal, Bhutan, Mongolia, and Russia, among other countries. These gorgeous cats have thick white fur with large black rosettes that help them hide along icy cliffs, which gives them the nickname "ghost of the mountains." This drink features vodka as a base with some Chinese baijiu and lychee, reflecting some of the spirits and fruits of the region.

**IF A MAN ASPIRES TOWARDS A RIGHTEOUS LIFE,
HIS FIRST ACT OF ABSTINENCE IS FROM INJURY TO ANIMALS.**

—ALBERT EINSTEIN,
GERMAN PHYSICIST

- 1½ ounces vodka
- ¾ ounce baijiu
- ¾ ounce yuzu puree
- ¾ ounce lychee liqueur
- Garnish: lemon twist

Shake all the ingredients with ice in a cocktail shaker and strain into a Martini glass. Lay the lemon twist on the rim of the glass.

Knock Me Down

While cheetahs are sometimes mistaken for leopards, these wildcats nearly all live in Sub-Saharan Africa. The fastest land animal on Earth, cheetahs have been recorded running up to 73 miles, or 117 kilometers, per hour within three seconds. Their long legs, elongated spine, and semi-nonretractable claws, which both grip and propel, make them incredibly powerful. Cheetahs tend to hunt during the day to avoid competing with other African big cats, such as lions, who hunt at night. The cheetah's attack often includes running quickly at a gazelle or warthog, taking it by surprise, and knocking it over. Once the prey is on the ground, the cat sinks its teeth into its victim's neck. Cheetahs are the only big cats that do not roar, and female cheetahs are solitary creatures other than when mating or raising cubs. In centuries past, cheetahs are said to have been trained by emperors and other royalty to help them hunt large deer. In captivity, cheetahs have lived up to 17 years. In the wild, their numbers are dwindling incredibly fast due to habitat loss and poaching. It is tragic to realize that 95 percent of cheetah cubs born will not survive. This drink is a strong, fiery shooter that you should enjoy with caution because you may not see the "pow" coming!

- ¾ ounce vodka
- ¾ ounce peppermint schnapps
- ¾ ounce cinnamon schnapps
- ¾ ounce chocolate liqueur
- ½ ounce high-proof rum

Shake the vodka, schnapps, and chocolate liqueur with ice in a cocktail shaker and strain into a rocks or Martini glass. Top with the high-proof rum. If desired—and you're feeling a little dangerous like our cheetah friends!—quickly strike a match and set the surface of the drink on fire. Caution should, of course, be taken and be sure to blow out the fire before drinking it!

Three of Cubs

Pumas are also known as cougars or mountain lions and are found throughout North, Central, and South America. These huge wildcats run at great speeds and are highly adaptable to mountains, jungles, grasslands, or even the desert. They are capable hunters both in daylight and at night. Pumas stalk large animals such as deer, moose, cattle, and horses, and when necessary, they feast on small rodents. They are distinguished by a black ring reaching from the corners of their mouth and around the nose, and can grow up to nine feet long, although average length is six to eight feet. They are usually yellowish but can sometimes be brown, gray, or reddish. They share a common ancestor with the African cheetah, and unlike African lions, pumas screech rather than roar. However, they are known to hiss and purr like the pet cats we know and love. And, like domesticated cats, their kittens are born with closed eyes. In early American history, pumas wandered across the continent, but Jesuit priests offered Native Americans one bull for every puma killed to encourage farming. A bounty system for hunting the cats continued in many states into the 1900s and, sadly, in the western states, they can still be hunted with a special license. Today, the only protected wildcats in this group within the United States are Florida panthers, whose population is slowly increasing. This drink highlights ingredients native to the Americas in honor of these stealthy animals.

- 1½ ounces mezcal
- 1½ ounces corn milk (Remove kernels from cob; blend until smoothie consistency; strain and save the liquid.)
- 1 tablespoon blueberries
- ½ ounce honey syrup
- ½ teaspoon sliced jalapeño
- Garnish: blueberries on a skewer

Shake all the ingredients with ice in a cocktail shaker and strain into a Martini glass. Place the skewered blueberries across the rim of the glass.

Treetops and Tropics

Jaguars are an ancient species of wildcat, which likely originated in Eurasia millions of years ago and crossed into the Americas during the Ice Age. They are the third largest in the world after lions and tigers, and there are 10 species of jaguar living all the way from the southern United States through Mexico and Central America down to Argentina. These solitary cats are fiercely territorial and only connect with others during mating season. Otherwise, they spend a fair amount of time alone in trees where they have safe sleeping quarters and a great vantage point from which they skillfully pounce on prey, large and small. They are also excellent swimmers, which serves them well in jungle environments where they sometimes even take down crocodiles. Jaguars are often yellowish with spots, but larger than African and Asian leopards. They were worshipped as gods in ancient South American cultures and are represented in much pre-Columbian art. Although they once wandered freely throughout what is now the United States, they are nearly extinct in North America due to habitat loss. In the areas of the Amazon being destroyed for cattle ranches, jaguars are routinely killed by ranchers and their population is severely threatened. They are also illegally killed because their teeth and bones are coveted in parts of Asia. As with all wildcats who are disappearing from the planet, nature lovers must fight against poaching and deforestation. The drink to honor this special animal features bold ingredients.

- 2 ounces Bourbon
- ¾ ounce fresh lime juice
- ¾ ounce orgeat syrup
- ¾ ounce blackberry liqueur
- Garnish: lime wheel

Shake all the ingredients with ice in a cocktail shaker and strain into a coupe or over fresh ice in a double rocks glass. Place the lime wheel on the rim of the glass.

I HAVE LIVED WITH SEVERAL
ZEN MASTERS—ALL OF THEM CATS.

—ECKHART TOLLE,
BEST-SELLING AUTHOR OF *THE POWER OF NOW*

CHAPTER
6

FAMOUS FELINES

WE KNOW THAT EVERY CAT IS MASTER OF THEIR OWN UNI-verse, headliner of their own show, and although they aren't pouring the shots in our home bars, they are often calling the shots in our homes. Judging by the many famous kitties we love to watch, read about, and laugh with, we just can't get enough feline star power. Authors, illustrators, and audiences alike are inspired and amused by cats' haughty attitudes, incredible physical talents, obvious intellect, and, quite frankly, downright cuter-than-should-be-legal appearance. Salvador Dalí, Georgia O'Keeffe, Andy Warhol, and Pablo Picasso are just a few painters known to keep cat muses while creating their masterpieces. We love to imagine what they are thinking, how they view us, and how we can best ingratiate ourselves to them. In short, we love cats, and kitty culture is celebrated all around us. This chapter highlights a few well-known felines and some of their backstories.

Bodhi Catfa

If you observe your own cat, it would not be difficult to imagine them meditating during the hours spent on a sunny windowsill, observing life from a distance. It may also be safe to assume that your cat is not emotionally attached to your happiness—or anything, really, other than a nice bowl of food. In his books, author David Michie shares amusing anecdotes through the eyes of a spiritual cat as she ponders some of life's deeper questions. The author weaves Buddhist philosophies through the adventures of this fictional Himalayan kitten rescued from cruel kids in the slums of New Delhi and lucky enough to land in a sacred temple in the mystical Himalaya mountains. She navigates life alongside a spiritual celebrity, meeting world-famous seekers, incorporating his lessons into her own way of thinking, and forging her own path toward enlightenment. Along the way, her challenges leave the reader with new insights to inner happiness, including learning to adapt rather than resist change and choosing how to react to the world rather than being controlled by difficult moments. I thought that a nod to a hot traditional Himalayan butter tea might be a nice way to toast this wise kitty, and I added an optional shot of whiskey to further raise our *spirits*!

- 4 ounces pu'er tea, brewed
- 1 ounce whiskey (optional)
- ¾ ounce cream (or nondairy cream)
- ¾ teaspoon butter (though yak butter is traditional, cow is more accessible!)
- ½ pinch Himalayan salt
- Garnish: pinch of ground cardamom

Whisk all the ingredients in a heat resistant bowl or pitcher. Pour into a bar mug and top with cardamom.

Cat-Man-Do Mornings

I know I'm not the only cat fanatic who scrolls through Simon's Cat online when looking for a happiness boost! English illustrator Simon Tofield introduced this massively popular, mischievous, and ever-hungry kitty to the world in an animated short film titled *Cat-Man-Do* around 2008. After it went viral on YouTube, he created a website. Soon, Simon's Cat was featured in books, comic strips, and gift items. A lifelong sketch artist and nature lover, young Simon was originally obsessed with drawing the birds who now make appearances in the *Simon's Cat* films. As he got older, the budding illustrator practiced animation by making flip-books and eventually got into creating TV commercials which he did for 13 years. He taught himself digital animation, and his first animated short was about his cat Hugh trying to wake him up to be fed. When this video went viral, the Simon's Cat empire was born. To this day, each *Simon's Cat* film is drawn by hand and takes a team of animators several months to complete. This drink is a tribute to the many cat lovers who relate to their furry friend not so subtly suggesting that it's time for breakfast!

- 1½ ounces London Dry gin
- 1 tablespoon orange marmalade
- ½ ounce fresh lime juice
- ½ ounce English breakfast tea syrup
- 1 egg white
- Garnish: dash of orange bitters on the frothy egg white

Dry-shake all the ingredients in a cocktail shaker. Then add ice and shake vigorously again. Strain into a coupe or Martini glass and dot the froth with bitters.

Lion's Mane

"Narnia, Narnia, Narnia, awake. Love. Think. Speak. Be walking trees. Be talking beasts. Be divine waters." These words were spoken by Aslan the Lion in The Chronicles of Narnia series. As creator of the magical world, Aslan is described as a wild lion who embodies goodness. Narnia is meant to reflect the mysterious land from whence he came, and Aslan populated it with a pair of talking animals of every kind. When the four children—Lucy, Edmund, Peter, and Susan—find their way there via a magical wardrobe, they also meet a plethora of mystical beings including centaurs, fauns, dwarves, and the evil White Witch. Aslan appears to guide the children in times of peril and even sacrifices his own life to save them before rising from the dead with the new dawn. The religious undertones of C. S. Lewis's book series are unmistakable, and the author was actually very open about them. The idea of a lion at the center of the story is said to have come to the author in a dream, and Aslan's physical appearance is modeled after a door handle at a church in Ireland where Lewis's grandfather was a vicar. Aslan is omnipotent and feared by the inhabitants of Narnia, but he is also comforting and leaves young readers longing to snuggle right into his great mane. Therefore, this drink, in honor of one of my personal favorite characters of all time, has a rich golden hue, packs some power, yet leaves a soft touch.

- 2 ounces gin
- ¾ ounce bitter Italian aperitif
- ½ ounce yellow French herbal liqueur
- Dash of bitters
- Garnish: orange twist

Stir all the ingredients with ice in a cocktail shaker and strain into a coupe. Garnish with an orange twist across the rim of the glass.

No-Name Slob

What cat lover could forget the scene in *Breakfast at Tiffany's* when Audrey Hepburn's character Holly Golightly professes to her boyfriend that she will not marry him: "I'm like Cat here. We're just a couple of no-name slobs. We belong to nobody and nobody belongs to us. We don't even belong to each other," and then she coldly tosses her cat out of the car into the pouring rain. Gasp! Of course, Hollywood gives us the ending we desire when she runs through the storm, full of regret, and pulls Cat out of a wet alley. (Yeah, sure, she makes up with the guy, too.) The actor portraying Cat was named Orangey, and he landed roles in many films at the time. He is said to have been a tad bad-tempered and bit actors occasionally, but who could blame him, really? Strangers were dousing him with water and forcing him to be on noisy movie sets. He was so freaked out that he sometimes ran away from the film crews, and one determined director kept dogs at the exits to ensure he couldn't escape. Orangey won two PATSY awards (Performing Animal Television Star of the Year), which is the equivalent of a feline Oscar, and was buried among movie royalty at Forest Lawn Cemetery in Los Angeles. This cocktail is made with orange-flavored blue curaçao in tribute to both Orangey the cat and the iconic little blue boxes containing precious baubles from Tiffany & Co. jewelry stores.

- 1½ ounces mandarin vodka
- ¾ ounce blue curaçao
- ¾ ounce fresh lemon juice
- Garnish: diamond ring *wink* (or orange slice)

Shake all the ingredients with ice in a cocktail shaker then strain into a coupe or over fresh ice in a double rocks glass. Add an appropriate garnish based on your annual cocktail budget.

Pink Martini

Often referred to as the "James Bond of the animation world," this Oscar-winning cool cat first appeared in the opening sequence of the Warner Brothers *Pink Panther* movie in 1963. Filmmaker Blake Edwards hired animation duo Hawley Pratt and Friz Freleng to come up with an animated character—he specified a pink panther—to promote his comedic film starring Peter Sellers as a bumbling Inspector Clouseau seeking the stolen "pink panther" diamond. Edwards also often collaborated with famed musician Henry Mancini, regarded as one of the greatest composers in the history of film, who dreamed up the iconic Pink Panther theme music. This rose-colored kitty went on to gain enormous fame as a Saturday morning cartoon for children in subsequent years. The obvious drink for this fastidious feline is a twist on the Vesper Martini—a vodka and gin variation made famous in a Bond movie—made with pink, slightly sweet sloe gin. And, unlike Bond, who had no reverence for a properly made Martini, this one is stirred, not shaken.

- 2 ounces vodka
- ¾ ounce sloe gin
- ½ ounce dry vermouth
- Dash of orange bitters
- Garnish: lemon twist

Stir all the ingredients with ice in a mixing glass for at least one minute until very cold. Strain into a Martini glass. Twist the lemon peel over the drink to express the oils and drop it in.

Wondrously Amusing

To "grin like a Cheshire cat" was a common saying around the time author Lewis Carroll first told the story of *Alice's Adventures Under Ground* to family friends in 1865. He expanded the story into a book in later years and adjusted the title to *Alice's Adventures in Wonderland*. The famous grinning phrase was supposedly used as far back as the 1700s and begs the question of just what those cats in Cheshire found so amusing? We can only speculate. In the story, though, this fantastical cat acts as a kind of spiritual guide, often leaving no trace of having been there other than his grand smile. When Alice is lost, pondering which way she should go to navigate the odd circumstances in which she has found herself, the cat responds: "That depends a good deal on where you want to get to." When she blurts out that she doesn't much care where she goes, the cat simplifies her dilemma by pointing out that, in that case, it doesn't really matter which path she chooses as she will wind up *somewhere* if she only walks long enough. The British tradition of afternoon tea is said to have begun among the aristocracy only a few decades before Carroll wrote this story, so the Mad Hatter's tea party is also a nod to its time. This fun drink draws inspiration from teatime along with a boozy component sure to bring a smile to your face.

- 2 ounces sweetened black current tea
- 1½ ounces Irish poitín (a kind of backcountry moonshine)
- 1 ounce cream liqueur
- Garnish: whipped cream and rainbow sprinkles

Shake all the ingredients with ice in a cocktail shaker and strain into a coupe. Top with whipped cream and sprinkles.

HOW TO MEET A CAT

Whether selecting a new feline family member at the shelter or getting introduced to your friend's pet, the way you approach a cat helps determine if you'll hit it off. The slow blink—slowly closing and opening your eyes—is cat language for "Hi! I'm harmless and friendly." You'll also notice that your cat touches noses with their other feline and canine buddies. If your cat wants to show you affection, offer your finger for a bump. When petting a new cat, bring your hand toward them from the side rather than from above to make them feel more comfortable. You may notice that cats also like to sit in high places where they can peruse the landscape. These are traits left over from ancient predecessors who were wary of overhead predators. And that whole thing about cats and boxes? It's another instinctive habit from living in rocky crags and hidey-holes where they were securely protected on all sides but could also peep out to stalk prey. Cats are so fascinating—and so particular—it's no wonder they are the subject of so many books, movies, and cartoons!

Hakuna Matata

The Swahili word for "lion" or "strength"—*simba*—became known the world over when the adorable timid lion cub turned brave leader in Disney's *The Lion King* was released in 1994. As part of his training to lead with compassion, Simba's father King Mufasa taught the cub to respect the circle of life, which means maintaining the balance between predator and prey. But when his greedy uncle Scar kills Simba's father to grab the throne for himself, Simba escapes to the desert where he meets a meerkat and warthog living the *hakuna matata* (no cares or worries) lifestyle. Eventually, his father's spirit calls upon him to reclaim his birthright at Pride Rock and free his lion family and the other animals suffering under Scar's evil rule. Simba goes through many challenges before eventually succeeding, and the lesson for us humans is undeniable. Mustering the courage to protect what is right is a theme in stories through the ages, and this one tells it beautifully. So a strong cocktail with a whisper of frivolity seems like the perfect combination to lead us to our own Hakuna Matata moment.

- 1 ounce spiced rum
- 1 ounce dark rum
- 1 ounce pineapple juice
- ¾ ounce elderflower liqueur
- ¾ ounce coconut milk
- ½ ounce fresh lime juice
- ½ ounce grenadine syrup
- Garnish: pineapple slice and cherries

Shake all the ingredients except the grenadine syrup with ice in a cocktail shaker and strain into a Collins glass or some other fun-shaped tall glass filled with fresh crushed ice. Pour the grenadine in last and it will slowly leak down into the rest of the drink creating a melting effect. Garnish with pineapple and cherries.

Schtroumpf-a-licious Azrael

Gen Xers and millennials are sure to remember the little blue plastic collectible characters known as Smurfs. Readers could follow the adventures of Papa Smurf, Smurfette, Brainy Smurf, and all the other personalities in the popular comic books by Belgian cartoonist Pierre Culliford, which were first published in French, in 1958. (In French, *smurfs* are *schtroumpfs*.) Among the characters is an evil wizard named Gargamel who has a clever kitty sidekick named Azrael. In the original comics, Azrael was a female cat, but in later animated films she was portrayed as male. The name Azrael means "angel of death" in several religions, but cat lovers can find the good in any kitty—even this one! After all, she was probably such a bitey and scratchy sort of guy because she was mistreated by the wicked Gargamel. If you've ever met an unfriendly cat, it's usually because they have endured some negative encounters with humans. Still, these two dysfunctional misfit characters were happier together than apart, and always wound up reunited in the end. This devilishly delicious drink has a bluish hue and interesting floral notes from the shochu and violet liqueur.

- 1½ ounces shochu
- 1 ounce half-and-half (or nondairy creamer)
- ¾ ounce crème de violette
- Garnish: powdered sugar

Rim a coupe with powdered sugar. Shake the liquor and half-and-half with ice in a cocktail shaker and strain into the rimmed glass.

Fanciful Wishes

Puss in Boots originates from an ancient fairy tale about a cunning cat who plots a scheme to win power and wealth. In that story dating back to 16th-century Italy, the feisty feline tricks a princess into marrying his human of humble beginnings, thus creating an alliance from which the cat benefits, too. As the anecdote of this clever kitty crept its way across Europe, a French version was published in the 1600s, and an English version later appeared in the stories of *Mother Goose*. Throughout time, however, tales of precocious pussycats duping people for their own gain appear in stories from Indian, Native American, and Asian cultures, too. Over the last few decades, Puss in Boots has sprawled into cartoons, films, and even a Tchaikovsky ballet. In the *Shrek* franchise, the Zorro-like, sword-wielding cat is voiced by Spanish actor Antonio Banderas, who also portrayed Zorro himself in his own films. This character is so loved by audiences that in 2022, the popular Puss got his own movie called *The Last Wish*. This drink uses Italian grappa and limoncello as a base with a swirl of French liqueur for a slightly romantic, sophisticated cocktail.

IN ANCIENT TIMES, CATS WERE WORSHIPED AS GODS; THEY HAVE NOT FORGOTTEN THIS.

—TERRY PRATCHETT,
ENGLISH AUTHOR

- 1½ ounces grappa
- ¾ ounce limoncello
- ½ ounce French orange liqueur
- ½ ounce fresh lemon juice
- ½ ounce honey syrup
- Garnish: edible flower

Shake all the ingredients with ice in a cocktail shaker and strain into a coupe. Float an edible flower on the surface of the drink.

I FEEL MUCH CLOSER TO NATURE AND ANIMALS THAN HUMANS.
. . . I ACCEPTED THE CAUSE OF ANIMALS TO FINALLY MAKE
SENSE OF MY EXISTENCE HERE. I'M TRYING TO EXPLAIN TO
MAN THAT CRUELTY INFLICTED ON ANIMALS IS UNWORTHY,
UNACCEPTABLE, [AND] INHUMANE . . .

—BRIGITTE BARDOT,
FRENCH ACTRESS

CAT LADIES
(AND GENTS!)

CATS MAY LOOK DOWN ON US FROM A LOFTY TREETOP PERCH,
a closet shelf, or simply down their noses with a haughty attitude but, ultimately,
they depend on humans for survival. Luckily, cat advocates come from all walks
of life, and despite the cat lady stereotype, men love felines as much as women
do. In this chapter, you'll meet some of the celebrities using their platforms to
help those who can't ask for help themselves. These friends in high places bring
awareness to dwindling wildcat populations as well as the plight of starving street
cats. For example, French feminist and liberated sex kitten Brigitte Bardot of the
fifties and sixties retreated from the limelight for the latter part of her life to create

her namesake rescue foundation. Today, her organization boasts four sanctuaries for all kinds of animals, takes legal action in cruelty cases across France, and still participates in CITES (Convention on International Trade in Endangered Species). Her friend and costar Alain Delon also often helped her efforts. Beloved culinary icon Julia Child was known for loving cats and helping to rehome strays. Her own Minou was sleeping aside her when she peacefully passed away at age 92. Today, Keanu Reeves is known as one of the most generous and compassionate humans in Hollywood largely because of his outspoken support of animal welfare. American bombshell Pamela Anderson is known for her many collaborations with PETA and musician Moby has "animal rights" tattooed on his arms. Being a high-profile celebrity makes it possible to lead by example because the world is watching and, often, admiring. This chapter celebrates just a few of the wonderful people who truly are a cat's best friend.

MUSIC TO CATS' EARS

British rock star Morrissey—front man for the 1980s new wave sensation the Smiths before becoming a solo artist—is a staunch animal advocate and PETA spokesperson. In fact, he is such a notable cat advocate that actor and fellow animal lover Russell Brand named one of his cats after *him*.

NO BAT WITHOUT A CAT

Nine actresses have sunk their claws into the iconic role of Catwoman from DC Comics' *Batman* series in adaptations for film and TV, starting with Julie Newmar in 1966, then Lee Meriwether, Eartha Kitt, Michelle Pfeiffer, Halle Berry, Anne Hathaway, Camren Bicondova, and Lili Simmons, all the way up to Zoë Kravitz taking on the role in 2022.

Bohemian Catsody

When asked if he'd like children one day, Queen's front man Freddie Mercury quipped that he'd rather have a cat. In fact, he had 10! Each cat had its own room in his London mansion, and each got its own Christmas stocking filled with treats. He also regularly called home to speak to his cats over the phone when touring the world. He dedicated his album *Mr. Bad Guy* "to my cat Jerry—also Tom, Oscar, and Tiffany, and all the cat lovers across the universe—screw everybody else!" He even wrote a song called "Delilah" in honor of the cat he referred to as his "little princess." In his final days, he spent hours painting her, and it is said that petting her was one of his last worldly pleasures before he died. The band's lead guitarist, Brian May, is also known for his feline affinity. He received acknowledgment from Queen Elizabeth II for "services to the music industry and charity work" as well as an award from the International Fund for Animal Welfare. This drink features English gin and has classic roots to honor these legendary rock stars and cat lovers.

- 2 ounces London Dry gin
- ¾ ounce dry vermouth
- ¼ ounce yellow herbal liqueur
- Garnish: dehydrated pineapple with a mini clothespin

Stir all the ingredients with ice in a cocktail shaker and strain into a coupe. Garnish with a dehydrated pineapple clipped to the side of the glass.

First Kitties

There have been several cats in the White House, which include President Abraham Lincoln's Tabby and Dixie, President George W. Bush's Willie, and President Bill Clinton's popular cat Socks. President Joe Biden and First Lady Dr. Jill Biden are known for their gorgeous German shepherds, but in 2022 a former farm cat named Willow made headlines as her carrier was loaded onto the Marine One helicopter on the White House grounds to join the family for a weekend at the shore. When in DC, a sign would alert staff to close doors stating, "Willow is on the prowl!" While animal lovers would like to see more protections for companion, farmed, and wild animals across the United States, this refreshing drink celebrates American heritage with a Bourbon base making it *purrfect* for the Fourth of July or an all-American backyard summer barbecue.

- 2 ounces ginger ale
- 1½ ounces Bourbon
- ¾ ounce fresh lemon juice
- ¾ ounce cranberry juice
- Garnish: American flag on a toothpick stuck into a few cherries

Pour all the ingredients into an ice-filled Collins glass and stir. Add an American flag with cherries to garnish.

Pickle Claps Back

Ricky Gervais loves animals and makes sure all his fans know it. He condemns animal abuse in his comedy shows, often posts his anticruelty sentiments on social media, and anyone following his Instagram knows he's quite smitten with his rescue kitty named Pickle. In his stand-up show *SuperNature*, he muses that his friends can't wrap their heads around how much he dotes on Pickle. That little snippet from the show became extremely popular with cat lovers across social media, and users uploaded videos of their own cats with Ricky Gervais's audio track clapping back at haters making fun of him spoiling his cat. Clearly, he's not the only one! The Pickle Back drink is a mixture of whiskey and pickle juice, and it was a popular unpretentious shot among bartenders for a hot minute when the fancy drink movement swung to extreme snobbery. Hopefully this version of the Pickle Back is slightly more palatable than the one guzzled in rebellious dive bars.

CATS POSSESS MORE SYMPATHY AND FEELING THAN HUMAN BEINGS.

—FLORENCE NIGHTINGALE,
BRITISH NURSE AND SOCIAL REFORMER WHO ADOPTED
MORE THAN 60 CATS DURING HER LIFETIME

- 1½ ounces whiskey
- ¾ ounce pickle juice
- Dash of Tabasco
- Dash of Angostura bitters

Shake all the ingredients with ice in a cocktail shaker and strain into a rocks glass over fresh ice or serve neat.

Whiskied Whiskers

Amanda Seyfried has compared fostering kittens with raising a baby and fellow fosterers are sure to agree. Round the clock feedings for these fragile felines are only part of what goes into helping them thrive. Seyfried understands the important role fostering plays because caring for needy animals in homes allows the shelter to admit more animals in need. She also brings the spotlight to animal welfare as an ambassador for Best Friends Animal Society's Save Them All campaign and has been honored by PETA for her outspoken advocacy. She and her husband, fellow actor Thomas Sadoski, and their children share the family farm with more than 20 rescued animals of various species. The actress is said to occasionally indulge in a nip of whiskey as liquid courage before talk shows—who could blame her!—so this original Scotch-based drink is created in honor of animal fosterers, like Amanda, who are the backbone of animal rescue.

- 1½ ounces Scotch
- ½ ounce artichoke liqueur
- ½ ounce sweet vermouth
- ½ ounce chocolate liqueur
- Garnish: chocolate shavings

Stir all the ingredients with ice in a cocktail shaker and strain into a coupe. Grate chocolate over the surface of the drink.

Gata Plata

Penelope Cruz is a self-proclaimed cat lady who quelled her loneliness in a new country by rescuing and fostering many cats when she moved to Los Angeles from Spain. She is also a passionate advocate against cruelty in the fashion world and has appeared in a PETA ad holding an orange tabby cat captioned, "Make us purr. Don't wear fur." Cruz went on to partner with Spanish clothing brand Mango, which declared itself fur-free in 2011, and launched her own cruelty-free fashion line for them with her sister Monica. Penelope and sultry Spanish hubby, actor Javier Bardem, have adopted many rescue cats and dogs and are known to even bring them along on interviews sometimes. This low-alcohol cocktail is a variation on a classic Martinez featuring sherry as the star and gin in a supporting role.

- 2 ounces Spanish sherry
- ¾ ounce Spanish gin
- ½ ounce cherry liqueur
- Dash of bitters
- Garnish: cherry

Stir all the ingredients with ice in a cocktail shaker and strain into a coupe. Drop in the cherry.

Nifty Swifty Kitty Kat Klub

Fans of Taylor Swift are well aware that she loves her cats. Just take a gander at her social media to peep at her fabulous furbabies. They also appear in her music videos, go on the road with her, and Taylor has been quoted as saying that they "are a joy to live with." The pop star considers her kitties dignified and independent, much like herself, to the point that she actually puts them to work. Her Scottish fold, named Olivia Benson, is reportedly worth nearly $100 million from online advertising. Taylor is also the kind of lady who puts her money where her whiskers are. She has made significant donations to many cat rescues including Beth's Furry Friends (see the Rescue Me! chapter, page 29). Taylor has no qualms about touting her preference for felines. When she adopted her third cat, she not-so-jokingly declared herself a cat lady. *Welcome to the club, Taylor!* This cocktail is sweet, soothing, and comforting enough to heal a broken heart, much like the lyrics of a Swift love song.

- 1½ ounces vanilla vodka
- 1 ounce chocolate liqueur
- ¾ ounce biscotti-flavored liqueur
- ¾ ounce cream
- Garnish: chocolate syrup and crumbs from a crushed chocolate cookie bar to make a rimmer

Wet the rim of a Martini glass with chocolate syrup, then roll it in the crushed cookie crumbs. Shake all the ingredients with ice in a cocktail shaker and gently strain into the rimmed glass.

Stay Cool

Acclaimed rapper and ASPCA award winner Sterling Davis has said that being a Black man in cat rescue is rare. The Atlanta-based advocate is known for touting, "You don't lose cool points for compassion." His tireless efforts to launch his own nonprofit called TrapKing Humane Cat Solutions are featured in the 2021 Netflix documentary *Cat People*. The organization's work focuses on TNR—or "trap, neuter, and release"—which helps the cat colonies in Los Angeles, Denver, Detroit, and Philadelphia, among others, by controlling stray cat populations rather than euthanizing them. His next goal is to expand his efforts overseas, starting with Greece, which is known for its many stray cats. Nothing is *cool*er than ice cream, and nothing is more attractive than being kind, so this boozy milkshake is sure to score points with Georgia peaches and kitty lovers everywhere.

- 3 ounces milk (or nondairy milk)
- 1½ ounces whiskey
- 1 ounce peach liqueur
- 1 big scoop peach ice cream (or any preferred flavor)
- Garnish: canned or fresh peach slices and a fancy, reusable straw

Blend all the ingredients in a blender to your desired consistency and pour into a Collins glass or any other big, fun glass. Top with peach slices and pop in a straw.

TIME SPENT WITH A CAT IS NEVER WASTED.

—SIDONIE-GABRIELLE COLETTE,
FRENCH AUTHOR AND ACTRESS

HAPPY PAWLIDAYS

ALL YEAR ROUND, OUR KITTIES MAKE US LAUGH, COO, AND cuddle up. They are part of our families and fabulous furry friends. Cats ask very little of us, really—a clean litter box, a never-ending supply of treats, food, water, and a warm lap. If you are a cat lover, you're likely to have friends who are too. So these kitty-themed cocktails are sure to be a hit at your next party! In this chapter, you'll find drinks based on our love for felines which are easy to concoct for celebrations throughout the year.

Lucky Cat

Marking a new year calls for cocktails no matter when you choose to celebrate. I also enjoy Chinese New Year when the calendar ticks over to a different animal in a 12-year cycle. Plus, I love the giant dancing dragon or lion in street parades! In the Vietnamese lunar calendar, the cat replaces the rabbit from the Chinese calendar, and people born in that year are said to be clever, creative, and ambitious as well as stubborn and self-indulgent. (Meow!) The lucky cat statuette appearing to give a high five seen in many Asian restaurants is originally from Japan and called maneki-neko. The Japanese New Year is often punctuated with a multiday party in the beginning of January. O-toso sake is a traditional drink during this time, so I created this cocktail using that particular sake and shochu (a popular Asian spirit), as well as some ingredients commonly found in Asian cuisine.

- 2 lychees, divided
- 1 teaspoon grated gingerroot
- 1 ounce shochu
- 1 ounce o-toso sake
- ¾ ounce green tea
- ½ ounce plum liqueur
- Garnish: black sesame seeds

Moisten the rim of a coupe, then dip it onto a plate of black sesame seeds. Set aside. Muddle one lychee with the ginger in the bottom of a mixing glass or cocktail shaker. Add the other ingredients and vigorously shake with ice. Gently double strain into the rimmed coupe to remove any bits of ginger. Drop the other lychee into the glass.

Purrrfect Pairing

Whether your perfect partner comes in human or feline form, Valentine's Day is all about the love! *Good Housekeeping* magazine reported that nearly 28 million Americans give Valentine's Day gifts to their dogs, and more than 17 million of us give them to our cats. Another study reveals that a third of pet parents would choose their pet over their partner if they had to pick one. (Are animal lovers really surprised?) Ideally, a love for animals is something every couple shares, and a pet makes their family feel complete. This cocktail is created to pair with a chocolate-covered strawberry, so whether you are imbibing with another human or just by yourself, it's a match made in heaven.

- 1½ ounces vodka
- ¾ ounce strawberry syrup
- ¾ ounce chocolate liqueur
- ¾ ounce cream
  (or coconut creamer)
- Garnish: chocolate-covered strawberry

Shake all the ingredients with ice in a cocktail shaker and strain into a Martini glass. Serve with a chocolate covered strawberry.

Catnip Julep

Spring is Julep season, so celebrate mama cat day with a unique, relaxing cocktail using both mint and catnip in this refreshing sipper. We all know the effects catnip has on our feline friends—they tend to get joyful, playful, and sleepy! Catnip contains nepetalactone, similar to valerian, which is used as an herbal sedative. It is in the mint family, along with basil and lemon balm, and can be brewed into a tea. This drink features fresh catnip leaves, so perhaps you'll want to grow some for both yourself and your kitty pals. As with any ingredients which aren't commonly used, please check with your doctor if you're unsure about utilizing catnip in your own food or drink, or simply leave it out and double the mint leaves. I've also added cherries to the mix as they are a wonderful early summer fruit. You can choose fresh, canned, jarred, or frozen, though, to make this yummy drink year-round. Muddle, sip, relax, and repeat throughout the warm months ahead.

- 10 mint leaves, no stem
- 10 catnip leaves, no stem
- 6–8 cherries, halved and pitted
- 1½ ounces Bourbon
- Splash of club soda
- ½ ounce mint syrup
- Garnish: extra sprigs of mint and catnip and a whole cherry

Muddle the leaves with the cherries in the bottom of a Collins glass or a metal Julep cup if you have one. Add the Bourbon, mint syrup, and a splash of club soda, then stir. Fill with crushed ice. Add in the herb sprigs for extra aromatics and top with a cherry.

CURL UP WITH CAT DADDIES

If you are looking for a movie for you and your kitty to enjoy over a holiday weekend, check out *Cat Daddies*. The documentary follows eight men and their feline friends during the early days of the 2020 pandemic and how the men's lives are forever changed by the special connections they developed with their cats. Pour yourself a cocktail and enjoy a fresh look at cat companionship and modern masculinity.

Kitty with a 'Tude

For some reason, people have assumed that cat enthusiasts skew female, but cat dads are plentiful and proud animal lovers, too! One of my favorite online cat dudes is Moshow the Cat Rapper. He lives in Portland, Oregon, with his many felines and uses his music, books, and very popular social media channels to inspire people to keep a positive "cattitude." He regularly posts photos with his cute kitties and brings awareness to the plight of rescue cats everywhere. In the United States, pretty much everyone celebrates the Fourth of July with barbecue and beer, but I thought this sudsy sipper in particular might lure more fellas into the cat-o-sphere of raising a delicious drink in honor of our furry friends, both online and in our own backyards.

- 6 ounces amber beer
- ¾ ounce rye whiskey
- Several dashes of smoky bitters (Check online or specialty stores for BBQ bitters and other smoky flavors.)
- Garnish: pickled green beans or carrots

Pour all the ingredients into a chilled bar mug or Collins glass. Place the pickled veggies on a pick across the rim of the glass or on a little plate alongside it.

Binx's Revenge

In the original movie *Hocus Pocus*, we witness the kidnapping of Emily Binx in 1693 by the evil Sanderson Sisters, and her brother Thackery setting out to save her. When Thackery finds the trio of witches concocting a spell to steal the young girl's spirit, he spills their cauldron, ruining their plan. As punishment, they turn him into a talking black cat who would live forever in the shadows, unrecognizable to his family and friends. Three hundred years later, Binx stumbles upon a young man named Max who accidentally brings the sinister sisters back to life. A whole lot of trouble ensues, and all looks lost when the witches get a hold of Binx again. This time, Max comes to his rescue, and things turn out well when Thackery's soul is released from his cat form as the evil sisters are finally destroyed for good. Well, after that roller-coaster ride, we all need a drink! This one can be made with or without alcohol, so it is suitable for all-aged guests at your Halloween party. (Serves 10–12 people.)

- 1 (750 ml) bottle nonalcoholic gin
- 2 cups cherry juice
- 2 cups orange juice
- ½ cup fresh lemon juice
- ½ cup cinnamon syrup
- Garnish: cinnamon sticks

Pour all the ingredients into a punch bowl. Ladle into ice-filled wineglasses or punch cups when serving. Garnish each drink with a cinnamon stick.

Nuts and Berries

The third Thursday in November has special meaning in the United States. While the Thanksgiving story originates with Native Americans and European settlers sitting down to a peaceful feast together, today, the overriding message is to make space for everyone to express gratitude as a source of peace, happiness, and the best mindset to appreciate every day. What are you thankful for? Among other things, I'm grateful for my many rescue animals whose furry little faces fill my home and heart with purpose. This festive drink brings together traditional flavors in a Thanksgiving meal and makes a delicious tipple for friends old and new—and their cats—to celebrate being together!

- 1½ ounces dark rum
- ¾ ounce hazelnut liqueur
- ½ ounce cranberry juice
- ½ ounce amaro
- Garnish: caramel sauce and crushed pistachio nuts

Dip the rim of a cocktail glass in caramel sauce then roll in crushed pistachios. Shake all the liquid ingredients with ice in a cocktail shaker and gently strain into the glass.

Tom and Jerry Punch

Chilly weather calls for indoor gatherings and drinks to warm us from the inside out. Similar to an eggnog, the classic Tom and Jerry punch originated in the United States. Around the holidays, in particular, it was ladled out in saloons and homes throughout the country. Some credit its creation to a British journalist living in the States in the 1820s who wrote a play featuring main characters Tom and Jerry and put together the drink to promote the show. The name of this drink may also bring to mind a popular Hanna-Barbera cartoon from the mid-1900s in which a mouse named Jerry is perpetually pursued by a cat named Tom. Animator John Carr won $50 for naming the cat and mouse duo after this boozy drink, which was extremely popular at the time. In vintage stores today, you may be lucky enough to find occasional cups and punch bowls with Tom and Jerry printed on them from that period. With the resurgence of cocktail culture, though, they have become scarce.

FOR THE BATTER:

- 12 eggs, separated
- 1 teaspoon cream of tartar
- 4 tablespoons unsalted butter, at room temperature
- ¾ cup raw sugar
- 2 ounces spiced rum
- 2 teaspoons vanilla extract
- 1 teaspoon ground cinnamon
- 1 teaspoon ground cloves
- 1 teaspoon ground nutmeg
- 1 teaspoon ground ginger

FOR THE DRINK:

- 1–2 tablespoons batter
- 1 ounce dark rum
- 1 ounce brandy
- 5–6 ounces hot whole milk, water, or both

To make the batter, beat the egg whites and cream of tartar until stiff and, in a separate bowl, whisk the egg yolks with butter and sugar until creamy, about five minutes. Mix the spiced rum, vanilla extract, and spices with the yolk mixture, then gently fold in the egg whites. Cover and refrigerate.

When serving individual drinks, ladle one to two tablespoons of the batter with the rum, brandy, and milk into a cocktail shaker. Shake vigorously with ice, then strain into punch cups or Martini glasses. To make a big batch of this recipe for a holiday party, use the batter recipe as the base, then translate "ounces" to "cups" for the liquids and mix them well in a punch bowl.

Good Night, Santa Claws

'Twas the night before Christmas and all through the house, the kitties were hunting and stalking a mouse! Okay, maybe my dark rendition of a famous poem is not the nicest way to get the kiddos to drift off to a peaceful sleep—but neither is the Icelandic legend about a scary Christmas cat who slinks around the wilds looking to gobble up children who aren't properly dressed for cold weather. Luckily, there are quite a few nice tales, too, including a medieval legend that recounts a litter of kittens being born in Bethlehem the same night as baby Jesus, suggesting that one became his pet. Another fun tale recounts a naughty kitty who nibbled at the holiday dinner. And, of course, all pet lovers' favorite author, veterinarian James Herriot, wrote a sweet story called *The Christmas Day Kitten*. Once the little ones are nestled snug in their beds, this cocktail is a perfect nightcap for the grown-ups to enjoy while snuggling up together and holding paws by the fire.

- 1½ ounces Calvados (French apple brandy)
- 1 ounce chocolate liqueur
- ¾ ounce sweet vermouth
- Dash of chocolate bitters
- Garnish: chocolate-covered cherry

Stir all the ingredients with ice in a cocktail shaker and strain into a coupe. Garnish with a chocolate-covered cherry.

In with the New!

Closing out a year reminds us that each day is a chance for a new beginning. We don't have to wait for the calendar to resolve to make our lives happier, healthier, and more meaningful. Whether you and your kitty are lounging at home while others are sweating on the dance floor or you're hosting a bash of your own, the start of a new year is a good time to show up in the world being more yourself than ever. Serving human friends a cocktail will make them happy for a few minutes, but being of service to furry friends in need will bring *you* happiness for a lifetime. Here's a bubbly toast to all the cats who need our help, and resolving to make the world a better place for them!

A KITTEN IS THE DELIGHT OF A HOUSEHOLD. ALL DAY LONG
A COMEDY IS PLAYED OUT BY AN INCOMPARABLE ACTOR.

—CHAMPFLEURY (JULES FLEURY-HUSSON),
FRENCH NOVELIST

- 4 ounces Champagne
- ¾ ounce prickly pear puree
- Garnish: anything that makes you happy

Pour half the bubbly into a coupe or white wine glass. Gently stir in the puree. Add the rest of the Champagne and garnish with a festive decoration of your choice.

OWNERS OF DOGS WILL HAVE NOTICED THAT, IF YOU
PROVIDE THEM WITH FOOD AND WATER AND SHELTER AND
AFFECTION, THEY WILL THINK YOU ARE GOD. WHEREAS
OWNERS OF CATS ARE COMPELLED TO REALIZE THAT IF YOU
PROVIDE THEM WITH FOOD AND WATER AND AFFECTION,
THEY DRAW THE CONCLUSION THAT *THEY* ARE GOD.

—CHRISTOPHER HITCHENS,
BRITISH AMERICAN AUTHOR AND JOURNALIST

COCKTAILS WITH YOUR CAT: CREATE A SIGNATURE DRINK

INTERNATIONAL CAT DAY TAKES PLACE ON AUGUST 8 EACH year. It was created by the International Fund for Animal Welfare, and people around the world participate by posting photos of their kitties on social media and raising money to help animal causes. But really, who needs an excuse to raise a glass to the furry friends who make every day of the year better? Maybe you would like to take it a step further? I've created countless signature cocktails for animal shelter fundraisers, high-profile events, and private parties, and I teach home bartenders how to craft their own drinks in The Liquid Muse live and online cocktail classes. So, in this section, you can practice what you've learned in this book. It's easier than you think to whip up a signature cocktail honoring your cat's birthday, their adoption anniversary or, well, just about any other occasion. Soon, you'll be cocktailing in honor of your cat—and perhaps some humans—like a pro!

Immortalizing your cat with a signature cocktail is a unique way to show your love for them. If you have never bartended or created a recipe before, don't worry. Personalizing a cocktail is simple when you start with a classic recipe and then swap out like-for-like ingredients. Think of cocktail making like cooking. For example, a chocolate chip cookie dough recipe will always have the same ratios of flour to salt to butter to eggs. That foundation doesn't change. However, the personalization happens when you swap butterscotch chips for chocolate or add pecans or make small adjustments. You can do the same with a cocktail recipe by switching out the base spirit, in the same proportion, for another one (e.g., replacing vodka with whiskey) or changing out the liqueur in an established drink with the same amount of a different liqueur. Below are some instructions and inspirations to point you in the right direction.

1. Pick your spirit. Do you love rum? Are you a whiskey aficionado? Is vodka your go-to? Start with the spirit you want to use as a base for your drink and work from there.

2. What are some of your favorite classic cocktails? Do you love Mai Tais? Manhattans? Cosmopolitans? Look up the original recipe and observe the ratios of spirit to other ingredients. Then experiment by replacing vodka with tequila or raspberry liqueur with chocolate liqueur.

3. What kind of glass will you use and how will it be served? Will it be up in a cocktail coupe? Poured over ice in a tall Collins glass?

4. What kind of garnish will you use to make your drink more impressive? A piece of fruit? A flower? A dehydrated orange wheel? Fancy ice?

5. When coming up with a name, consider the following for inspiration: What is the name of your kitty? How would you describe their personality? What style of drink are you making? (Tropical? Sophisticated? Classic? Inspired by a film or character?)

Let these directions help you get shaking and impressing your pals in no time. Or maybe you'll toast your favorite feline while curled up on the sofa, just the two of you. As we cat lovers know, anything is more fun with your furry companion by your side. So let's raise a glass to you and your cat and the special time you share together!

Acknowledgments

This book would not have come to life without our talented (all-female) publishing team: my agent Lilly Ghahremani, my editor Jordana Hawkins, our designer Frances Soo Ping Chow, our production editor Amber Morris, our copy editor Ashley Benning, and our illustrator Rae Ritchie.

Index

About
the Author

Natalie Bovis is an award-winning mixologist, event producer, author, and founder of The Liquid Muse. She created TACO WARS and is the cofounder of OM Chocolate Liqueur and New Mexico Cocktail Week. She produces retreats, culinary festivals, and special dinners for clients including the James Beard Foundation. Natalie has volunteered with many animal rescues over the years, and part of her personal mission is raising money for animal advocacy groups. She teaches cocktail and cooking classes and has shaken up cocktails and mocktails on television shows across the United States. Natalie is the American-born daughter of an English mum and French dad and has lived and worked in Santa Fe, Los Angeles, Paris, Washington, DC, and the Costa Brava in Spain. Her passions include protecting wildlife and the environment, traveling, cooking, hiking, and writing articles, poetry, fiction, and nonfiction. Her previous cocktail books include *Preggatinis: Mixology for the Mom-to-Be, The Bubbly Bride: Your Ultimate Wedding Cocktail Guide, Edible Cocktails: From Garden to Glass*, and *Drinking with My Dog: The Canine Lover's Cocktail Book*. Share more cocktail fun with Natalie at TheLiquidMuse.com or @theliquidmuse on social media channels.